INTERNATIONAL ECONOMIC RELATIONS

International Economic Relations

GAUTAM MURTHY

PUBLICATIONS

KALPAZ PUBLICATIONS

DELHI-110052

International Economic Relations

Rs. 650

ISBN: 81-7835-615-5

Published in 2008 in India by
Kalpaz Publications
C-30, Satyawati Nagar,
Delhi-110052
E-mail: kalpaz@hotmail.com
Phone : 9212729499

Lasser Type Setting by: Quick Media, Delhi
Printed at : Vishal Kaushik Printers Delhi

CONTENTS

FOREWORD

This Book by Dr. Gautam Murthy is a timely addition to the literature on "International Economic Relations". I have known him for the past five years, and am quite familiar with his academic writings and views on global issues. He has extensively worked and researched on ASEAN, SAARC and East Asian issues, particularly those with an economic dimension. Dr. Murthy has a very good understanding of international issues, both from a strategic and diplomatic perspective. He has made strategic interventions in many national and international conferences, which were widely appreciated. Dr. Murthy is one of the new breed of South Asian scholars, who has shown pragmatism in his work, and has not failed to take into account new dimensions in India's foreign policy. He has provided useful insights and inputs to both academicians as well as policy formulators. I rate his academic contribution highly.

A.N. RAM

Formerly Secretary (East), Ministry of External Affairs,
Government of India,
Ambassador of India to the European Union, and Thailand, and Chairman, CSCAP (Conference on Security and Cooperation in Asia and Pacific (India Chapter).

ACKNOWLEDGEMENTS

I would like to place on record my deep appreciation to certain individuals who have helped me over the years, both professionally and personally. At the very outset I would like to thank Prof. Rama Melkote, Former Director of the Centre for Area Studies (now known as Centre for Indian Ocean Studies), for being instrumental in my professional growth at Osmania University, and always giving me a patient hearing in times of academic crisis. Dr. Charan D Wadhva, Emeritus Professor at the Centre for Policy Research, New Delhi, and Former R.B.I. Chair Professor at the Indian Institute of Management, Ahmedabad, always gave me full academic support over the last 30 years, and congratulated me whenever my Articles were published. Prof. B.S.R. Rao, Director of the International Institute of Insurance and Finance (IIIF), Hyderabad and Formerly R.B.I. Professor at Gokhale Institute of Politics and Economics, Pune (G.I.P.E.) encouraged me academically in my formative years, when I was Researching for my Ph.D. at G.I.P.E. Fr.T.A. Mathias, SJ former Dean of XLRI, Jamshedpur, was always appreciative of my academic creativity, when I was on the Faculty of XLRI.I would like to place on record the help and support I received from many individuals at Institutions I have served in-Osmania University (O.U.)-I Owe a Lot to You! for giving me both bread and butter; my colleagues and student friends at XLRI, Jamshedpur, and and, G.I.P.E., Poona-who made life more enjoyable. I would also like to thank the Library Staff at O.U., and the Secunderabad Club, for assisting me on many occasions.

I would like to immensely thank my dear wife, Mrs. Mayura Murthy, who has been my constant source of inspiration over the last decade. I owe everything to her, and my life would be incomplete without her constant support and encouragement.

ACKNOWLEDGEMENTS

1

REGIONAL TRADING BLOCKS, STATIC AND DYNAMIC EFFECTS OF CUSTOMS UNIONS AND FREE TRADE AREAS (FTAs)

Introduction

Regional cooperation is a more 'general' term than integration, where two or more countries come together for mutual benefit. It takes the form of:

1. Technology transfer
2. Sharing managerial expertise
3. Joint production and marketing facilities
4. Pure commodity trade

Economic integration is a 'narrower term'. The term was first used in the field of "industrial organization", meaning a combination of business firms through agreements, cartels trusts and mergers. RTAs are Regional Trading Agreements. The motivating factors for forming RTAs are:

RTAs (Regional Trading Agreements)

1. Regional cooperation can be effective in exploiting regional complementarities and economies of scale.
2. Regional cooperation by bringing about diplomatic cohesion, can reduce regional tensions, and effectively keep out negative extra – regional influences.
3. Regional cooperation can lead to industrial restructuring, and a more effective and efficient production structure within individual countries.

4. Smaller countries get increased "security of market access", and "safe havens" by forming RTAs.
5. Unilateral domestic policy reforms can be locked in once RTAs are formed.
6. Countries in RTAs can improve their bargaining power in Multilateral Trade Negotiations (MTNs).
7. Industries can be promoted that are not viable, without protected regional markets - Regional infant industries - the idea being that they would be internationally competitive if given sufficient time to develop.
8. RTAs can offer a quicker solution for free world trade, than multilateralism, which is much slower.
9. Article XXIV of WTO says that RTAs are constraint with globalization.
10. Intra-regional trade liberalization increases competition for regions within industries, improving technical and business complementarity and also attracts Foreign Direct Investment (FDI).

The terms RTAs (Regional Trading arrangements) and FTAs (Free Trade Aeras) can be used interchangeably.

Stages in Integration

There are various stages in the integration process, and levels of cooperation and integration among the participating countries. These are:

1. PTAs or Preferential Trade Arrangements. Quantitative restrictions and tariffs between participating countries are 'reduced' not 'abolished'.
2. FTAs or the Free Trade Areas, where quantitative restrictions, and tariffs between countries 'are abolished' - but where each participant country retains its own tariffs against non-members.
3. Customs Union where the participating countries impose the same tariffs on non-members i.e., Common External Tariff (CET)

4. Common Market, where restrictions on factor movements are abolished, i.e., services and labour movement, within the integration area flow freely.
5. Economic Union – Monetary policies are harmonized, like a common currency in the EU (European Union). Economic ad social policies are to some extent harmonized.
6. Supra-national Union – Governments of participating countries relenquish their sovereignty even over defence and foreign policies to a supra-national authority. This has happened to some extent in the European parliament, but as the Iraq was has demonstrated, there are deep divisions even in Europe over defence and foreign policy objectives.

Customs Union

A Customs Union generally promotes economic welfare. Jacob Viner however shows that this may not be totally correct. A customs union, combines elements of free trade with elements of protection, and may either improve or worsen resource allocation and welfare, depending whether trade creation or trade diversion take place. A customs union has both Static and Dynamic Effects.

Static effects refer to certain developments like increased competition, stimulus to technological changes, stimulus to investment and increased economies of scale that make the union economy more dynamic.

There are two types of Static Effects, namely., (*i*) Production effects and (*ii*) Consumption effects. Viner shows us the production effects. Production effects refer to the changes in the sources of supply or production bases of a commodity resulting from the formation of the customs union.

Trade Creation and Trade Diversion

Viner distinguished between two types of production effects – trade creation and trade diversion. Trade creation refers to the beneficial effect of the customs union of shifting supply from a high-cost domestic source to a lowest-cost source of another member of the union. Customs unions result in creation of fresh opportunities for trade. Trade diversion refers to the diversion of trade in a commodity from one country to another as a result of the formation of a customs union.

Thus, trade creation refers to newly created trade between member countries of the customs union, whereas trade diversion refers to some old trade being diverted from a foreign country to a member country, consequent upon the formation of the customs union. Trade creation adds to welfare, while trade diversion is against welfare. Trade creation improves international allocation of resources by shifting the source of supply from a high-cost producer to a low-cost producer. Trade diversion, however, worsens international allocation of resources by shifting supply sources to high-cost producers from low-cost producers.

Dynamic Effects

The dynamic effects of the customs union refer to some developments that increase economic efficiency of resource utilization. The important dynamic effects are increased competition, economies of scale stimulus to technical change and stimulates to investment. The dynamic effects of forming a customs union are far more important than the static effects.

Indian FTAs

India has FTAs with SAARC, Singapore and Thailand - similar arrangements are to be signed with ASEAN, Japan, China and South Korea. With Singapore, a CECA (Comprehensive Economic Cooperation Agreement) has been signed. This is more than an FTA, as the agreement includes services and investments also, which benefits both sides more. The political significance of trade pacts is more than the economic factors, hence the move to go in for CECAs with Sri Lanka, and Mauritius as well.

India was working on concluding FTAs with the ASEAN, Japan and China. A web of engagements with Asian Countries, Australia and New Zealand in the South Pacific will create and maintain a regional and international environment conducive to maintenance of high economic growth. Steps should be taken to ensure that savings and surpluses generated in the region find investment avenues within the region. An Asian Community should offer competitive complementary markets. However, FTAs affect domestic farmers adversely, instead of opening up agricultural and manufacturing sectors. Through FTAs more effective domestic policy measures need to be adopted to protect and strengthen growers and manufacturers.

2

PROBLEMS AND PROSPECTS OF FORMING UNIONS IN THE ASIAN REGION, SAARC/SAPTA AND ASEAN

Introduction

Asian developing countries have made a number of attempts at regional cooperation in the 1970s, with UN ESCAP's (Economic and Social Commission of Asia and Pacific) initiative. These include the Bangkok Agreement, established in 1975, which covered exchange of tariff concessions between five (5) member governments viz., Bangladesh, India, Laos, South Korea and Sri Lanka. The Asian Clearing Union (ACU) with seven members in the region, viz., Bangladesh, India, Iran, Myanmar, Nepal, Pakistan and Sri Lanka come into being in 1974. These early experiences have not been very successful. The Bangkok Agreement, suffered from the limited coverage of membership, as well as products covered and preference margins were not deep enough, and scope not extending to non-tariff barriers.

Territorial Ambit of Asia

Asia is essentially a geographical expression. It covers the Arabic – speaking countries in West Asia, Israel, Turkey and Iran. South Asia includes Afghanistan and SAARC countries (Afghanistan will become a member of SAARC in 2007). SAARC includes India, Bhutan, Nepal, Pakistan, Bangladesh, Sri Lanka and the Maldives. South-east Asia includes ASEAN (Indonesia, Malaysia, the Philippines, Singapore, Thailand, Brunei Sultanate, Vietnam, Laos, Myanmar, and Cambodia). East Asia groups China, the Korean Peninsula and Japan. These countries constitute a variety of ethnic groups, languages and faiths. Historically, there has been no evolution of an "Asian entity" or an "Asian identity". This is in marked contrast to the unifying embrace of a Hispanic identity, which brings the people of South and Central America together, a Caribbean identity, an African identity, a North American identity and a European identity. This sense of a shared identity has already found institutional expression in the European Union (EU), the Organization of American States, or the African Union (AU).

Asia is a region of "multiple heterogeneities" - namely geographical, economic, political and social. The region does not lack resources, but lacks initiatives for building complementarities. A closing of the ranks in the whole of Asia, will ensure greater reciprocity in economic relations with Europe and North America.

It is only in the last few years of the last century and more so in the present century that one talks of a unified "Asian identity" or on "Asian century". The Asian countries will also now include the Asian Republics of the former Soviet Union. Even today, when we talk of an "Asian Century", we include only ASEAN, China, Japan, Korea and India. West Asia, Central Eurasia (countries of the former Soviet Union), and other SAARC countries are ignored. The growth potential of Asia derives from the large and diversified natural resource base and productive structures in the region. Its member countries produce everything from energy, vital minerals, tropical products, fibres and cereals. It covers industrial and trading capacities ranging from the most labour-intensive to the most capital-intensive, with a large and varied workforce commanding different compensation levels. All these factors are highly conducive to greater economic interaction.

Major Regional Organizations in Asia are:

1. *SAARC (South Asian Association for Regional Cooperation)* Established in 1985. Will include Afghanistan in 2007, with China and Japan as observers.
2. *ASEAN (Association for Southeast Asian Nations)* The original signatories of ASEAN declaration at Bangkok signed in 1967 were Indonesia, Malaysia, the Philippines, Singapore

and Thailand. Brunei become a member in 1984. In mid-1985, Vietnam gained admission as the seventh member of ASEAN. Laos and Myanmar followed suit two years later in 1997, and Cambodia joined in 1999. Thus ASEAN today has 10 members, covering all countries of South east Asia from Myanmar in the extreme West, to Vietnam in the extreme East.

3. *IOR-ARC (Indian Ocean Rim Association for Regional Cooperation)* It was formed in 1997, and has 19 countries as members. The three key players are Australia, India and South Africa. It is based on the principle of "Open Regionalism". Its members are drawn voluntarily, and conditions of membership are on "non-binding commitments". It has been a regional non-starter, too diverse in membership of countries, geographically scattered members and no interaction taking place. The areas of voluntary action are :

   1. Trade liberalization,

   2. Trade facilitation and

   3. Investment facilitation.

   Sectoral cooperation projects also play a role in open regional arrangements .

4. SCO (Shanghai Cooperation Organisation) – China, Russia and five Central Asian Republics are members (Kyrgyzstan, Kazakhstan, Turkmenistan, Tajikistan and Uzbekistan). Pakistan, Iran and India are observers. It is a new regional organization binding Russia, China and the newly liberated Soviet Republics through economic engagement.

   Today, over 60 per cent of world trade is routed through RTAs or PTAs, and only around 40 per cent through the multilateral or MFN (Most Favoured Nation) process. It must be noted here that the terms RTAs (Regional Trading Arrangements), PTAs (Preferential Trading Arrangements) and FTAs (Free Trade Areas) are used inter-changably.

Details of SAARC

The South Asian Association for Regional Cooperation (SAARC) is a manifestation of the determination of the people of South Asia to work together towards finding solutions to their common problems in a spirit of friendship, trust and understanding. It was established to crate an order based on mutual respect, equity and shared benefits. SAARC was established at Dhaka on December 8, 1985.

The first Summit of SAARC was held at Dhaka, the capital of Bangladesh in 1985. The second SAARC Summit was held at Bangalore, India on November 17, 1986. The third SAARC summit was held at Katmandu, Nepal on November 4 1987. The fourth summit was held at Islamabad, Pakistan on December 31, 1988. The fifth summit was held at Male capital of Maldives on November 23, 1990. The sixth summit was held at Colombo, capital of Sri Lanka on 21 December, 1991. The seventh summit was held in Dacca (second time in Dhaka) on 1 April 1993. The eighth SAARC summit was held at New Delhi, capital of India on 4 May 1995. The ninth SAARC summit was held at Male, Maldives (second time at Maldives) on 14 May, 1997. The tenth SAARC summit was held at Colombo, Sri Lanka (second time at Colombo) on 31 July, 1998. The eleventh SAARC summit was held at Kathmandu, Nepal (second time at Kathmandu) on 4 January 2002. The twelfth SAARC summit was held at Islamabad, Pakistan in 2004. The thirteenth SAARC summit was held at Dhaka in December, 2005.

The basic aim of SAARC is to accelerate economic growth, social progress and cultural development in the region, and to promote and strengthen collective self-relevance among the members. The SAARC countries have various common economic features such as poverty, income inequality, large populations, low productivity, illiteracy, and unemployment. One-third of the population of the region lives below the poverty line. The region accounts for 21.7% of the world population and 3.4% of the total land area, but only a small share – 1.9% of the world output.

Trade should be a major priority area of SAARC economic countries. In spite of this, their intra-regional trade has been less than 5% of their global trade.

SAARC countries have succeeded in establishing SAPTA (SAARC Preferential Trading Area) in December 1995 and SAFTA (SAARC Free Trade Area) in 2001. The ultimate goal is to form SAARC Economic Union (SEU), on the pattern of the European Union (EU).

In spite of the operationalization of SAPTA, SAARC countries have been continuing with existing tariff structures.

ASEAN—Objectives of ASEAN

The ASEAN Secretariat is in Jakarta, the capital of Indonesia. The official language is English. The objectives of ASEAN are—(*i*) Economic, social and cultural development of the sub-region; (*ii*) Promotion of peace and stability in the sub-region, (*iii*) Encouragement of cooperation and mutual assistance in areas of common interest, (*iv*) Cooperation in economic, social, cultural, technical, scientific and administrative fields. (*v*) Mutual aid in education, professional and vocational training and administration through the provision of training and research facilities; (*vi*) Cooperation to develop agriculture and industry, to expand trade to develop transport and communication, and to raise the standard of living of inhabitants of the sub-region and (*vii*) Cooperation with international, regional and extra-regional organizations.

Structure of ASEAN

The organizational structure of ASEAN includes:

(*i*) Meeting of ASEAN Heads of State and Government

(*ii*) ASEAN Ministerial Conferences

(*iii*) Senior Economic Officials Meeting (EOM)

(*iv*) ASEAN Secretary General and Secretariat.

After the ASEAN annual summit there is a Post-Ministerial Conference (PMC) with its dialogue partners and an ASEAN Regional Forum (ARF) of 23 members that seeks to address security issues in the Asia-Pacific Region. ARF met for the first time in 1994. ASEAN has a plus three dialogue with China, Japan and South Korea, and an independent summit with India since 2001.

ASEAN had limited cooperation on economic issues until 1992, when it was decided to set up the AFTA (ASEAN Free Trade Area). AFTA is to be established by 2008.

The main mechanism for implementation of AFTA is the CEPT (Common Effective Preferential Tariff). CEPT tariffs were reduced between 0% to 5% by 2003 for the ASEAN 6%. The deadline for Vietnam is 2006-07.

There has been a marked increase in intra-ASEAN trade. Total intra-ASEAN trade increased from 18% in 1992 to 25% 2005.

ASEAN has also emerged as a major force in international relations with the ARF given great importance by all great powers, including China, the US, Russia and Japan. The recently concluded high-profile EAS (East Asian Summit) also drew world-trade attention.

India-ASEAN Linkages

India has moved purposefully in developing a broad economic and strategic partnership with the dynamic countries of South East Asia.

Chronology

1991 – India's engagement with ASEAN started with its "Look East" Policy.

1992 – India became a sectoral dialogue partner of ASEAN, cooperating in trade, investment and tourism.

1996 – India become a full dialogue partner and an active participant in the ARF. ARF met for the first time in 1994.

2001 – ASEAN - India relationship upgraded to the summit level.

2002 – First ASEAN - India summit in Phnom - Penh

2003 – Second ASEAN - India Summit in Bali, concluded with the signing of 3 major documents. These were:

(*i*) Framework agreement for comprehensive economic cooperation

(*ii*) Accession document to the TAC (Treaty of Amity and Cooperation) (*iii*) Adoption of Joint declaration on cooperation in combating international terrorism.

2004 – Third ASEAN - India Summit in Vientiane, capital of Laos. Agreement on "India – ASEAN partnership for Peace, Progress and shared Prosperity.

2005 – Fourth ASEAN - India Summit in Kuala Lumpur, Malaysia. India's high profile role established in the East Asia Summit with, ASEAN, Japan, Korea, China, Australia and New Zealand (16 countries).

The India – ASEAN Free Trade area is likely to come into force in 2007.

India has an FTA with Thailand, and a CECA (Comprehensive Economic Cooperation Agreement) also been signed with Singapore in 2005.

There are also two other sub-regional partnerships which India has in the ASEAN region. These are:

(*i*) MGC – Mekong – Ganga Cooperative Forum. It is a Cooperative forum floated by India with five of its Eastern neighbours – Myanmar, Thailand, Cambodia, Vietnam and Laos in 2001. Tourism, culture and education are given precedence and priority in the cooperative forum. Transport, communication, and infrastructure are next areas of priority.

(*ii*) BIMSTEC (Bay of Bengal initiative for Multi-Sectoral Technical and Economic Cooperation). First summit was held in Bangkok in July 2004. Part of India's immediate and intermediate neighbourhood policy is addressed in this forum. It includes – India, Bangladesh, Bhutan, Myanmar, Thailand, Nepal, Cambodia, Vietnam and Laos.

The Mekong basin has the potential to engage as a major grannary, as its vast lands are very fertile India and Thailand an do much to trame the Mekong river, and enhance cultivation by spreading irrigation.

Closer economic and political interaction with the economically dynamic group of countries like ASEAN, will motivate our decision makers to effect much needed changes in economic institutions, and policies, to make the economy vibrant, and foreign policy more dynamic.

Update on SAFTA

India and Pakistan have agreed not to levy import duties of more than 5% on products traded within SAFTA. The other five SAARC countries have also agreed to reduce their import duties by between 0% and 5% within the next 10 years. SAFTA will be totally effective only by 2016. Intra-regional trade volume among SAARC counties stands at $6 billion, or a mere 4.4% of the total trade of member states, worth $35 billion. This is in contrast to intra-regional trade of 55% in the EU, 61% in NAFTA, and 25% in ASEAN. Pakistan's "positive list approach" regarding items, which could be imported from India is the biggest obstacle to normal direct trade relations with India. Even if Pakistan does not give full MFN status to India, it is not economically rational for Pakistan not to put on the positive list goods that it at present imports from other countries. Such an arrangement would introduce an element of fair competition that will benefit the Pakistani consumer and importer. If SAFTA is implemented in letter and spirit, bilaterally traded goods could be brought back into the Indo-Pakistani ambit. In the indirect (unofficial trade) estimated to be US $2.5 billion, higher transportation costs make many potential Pakistani commodity exports to India uneconomical Transit – facilitation needs to also be implemented if Peshawar becomes the hub of India's trade with Afghanistan and Central Asia.

3

EUROPEAN UNION (EU), NORTH AMERICAN FREE TRADE AREA (NAFTA) AND WORLD TRADE ORGANIZATION (WTO)

The forerunner of the European Union (EU) was the European Coal and Steel Community, established in the early 1950s. This evolved into the European Economic Community (EEC) also known as the European Common Market (ECM) or the European Community (EC), and now as the European Union (EU). It is the most successful of regional economic integration schemes.

The EEC, originally comprised six nations – Belgium, France, Federal Republic of Germany, Italy, Luxembourg and the Netherlands – came into being on January 1, 1958 by the virtue of the Treaty of Rome of 1957. The EEC was expanded in 1973, with the inclusion of the UK, Denmark and Ireland. Greece joined the community in 1981, Spain and Portugal became members in 1986. Austria, Finland and Sweden also joined the EC later the membership rising to 15. Today the EU has 25 members, including some countries, of the former Soviet Bloc in Eastern Europe, and some of the newly liberated countries of the former Soviet Union.

The objectives of the formation of the EU as envisaged in the Treaty of Rome are:

(i) Elimination of tariffs, quotas and other barriers on intra – community trade,

(ii) Having a common internal tariff on imports from the rest of the World,

(iii) Allowing the free movement of factors of production within the community,

(iv) Harmonising of taxation and monetary policies, and also social security policies, and

(v) Adopting a common policy on agriculture, transport and competition in industry.

Indo-EU Trade

The EU, taken as a single unit is India's largest trading partner. India's main exports to the EU include textiles, jute, leather and leather goods, polished diamonds engineering goods, chemicals, and marine products. Imports include edible oils, fertilizers, dairy products, steel, capital goods, optical instruments, aluminian and copper products, synthetic rubber, photo and cinema equipment. India also receives technology investment and development from the EU countries.

India's export performance to EU has been rather poor. Lack of price competitiveness, poor quality, poor reputation with respect to delivery schedules, inadequate export marketing skills, and protectionist policies of the EU countries, are the main factors for a sluggish growth in India-EU trade, particularly India's exports to EU. India should pay great attention to the emerging opportunities in the EU, and improve quality of exports and stick to delivery schedules.

North American Free Trade Agreement (NAFTA)

The 1988 accord between the United States and Canada to drop all trade barriers was extended to Mexico, forming a North America Free Trade Agreement (NAFTA), making North America a giant free trade area. U.S. companies will immensely benefit by shifting production to Mexico, where labour is substantially cheaper, as compared to the US. NAFTA will result in free movement of American capital to Mexico – a better alternative from the US view point, when compared to the free movement of Mexican labour to the US. Environmentalists have also expressed concern about the US moving highly polluted industries to Mexico, which has less stringent environment protection laws.

NAFTA would eliminate all tariffs on products moving among the three countries, and other barriers to services and investment capital within North America. NAFTA would be a unified market to rival the EU.

World Trade Organisation (WTO) – Background

The WTO is the only international body dealing with the rules of trade between nations. At its heart are the WTO agreements, negotiated and signed by the bulk of the World's trading nations. The WTO was established in 1995, as part of the Uruguay Round of Trade Negotiations. The three main purposes of WTO are:

1. To help trade flow as freely as possible,
2. To provide a forum for trade negotiations, and
3. Settling trade disputes – The dispute settlement mechanism.

GATT and WTO

For several decades, GATT (General Agreement on Tariffs and Trade) was applied on a provisional basis. It was a multilateral agreement containing rules relative to trade in goods, and although it operated like a permanent agreement, it was without a permanent institutional framework, and was serviced by an ad hoc secretariat. The WTO now provides a permanent institutional framework for the multilateral trading system, with its own secretariat. In addition the WTO not only covers trade in goods, as the GATT rules did, but also trade in services, and trade-related aspects of IPRs (Intellectual Property Rights). Also, the dispute settlement mechanism has been considerably strengthened in the WTO.

Objectives and Functions of WTO

In the preamble of the Marrakesh Agreement establishing the WTO, the parties to the agreement recognize certain objectives to which they wish to contribute through the multilateral trading system. It is recognized that Member's relations in the field of trade and economic endeavor, should be conducted with a view to raising standards of living, ensuring full employment and a large and steadily growing volume of real income, and effective demand and expanding the production of and trade in goods and services, while allowing for the optimal use of the world's resources in accordance with the objectives of sustainable development. The WTO agreement also recognizes the need for "positive efforts" to ensure that LDCs, and especially the least developed among them, secure a share in the growth in international trade commensurate with the needs of their economic development.

The main functions of the WTO are:

1. To administrator WTO trade agreements.
2. To provide a forum for trade negotiations.
3. To handle trade disputes.
4. To monitor national trade policies.
5. To provide technical assistance and training for LDCs.
6. To cooperate with other international organizations.

Background of the formation of WTO – GATT Rounds

During the period, 1947 to 1993, the contracting parties successfully concluded eight rounds of trade negations. These eight rounds are listed below, with the years in which they were held.

1947 – The birth of General Agreement on Tariffs and Trade (GATT). The GATT was signed by 23 countries. The agreement contained tariff concessions agreed during the first multilateral trade negotiations, and a set of rules designed to prevent these concessions from being frustrated by restrictive trade measures.

1949 – Second Round at Annecy France. The contracting parties exchanged some 5,000 tariff concessions.

1950-51 – Third Round at Torque, U.K. The contracting parties exhcnaged some 8,700 tariff concessions, yielding tariff reductions of about 25 per cent in relation to the 1948 level.

1956 – Fourth Round at Geneva. The round produced 82.5 billion worth of tariff reductions.

1960-62 – Dillon Round. Named in honour of the U.S. Under – Secretary of State, Douglas Dillcn, who proposed the negotiations, the fifth Round was divided into two phases. The first was concerned with negotiations, which resulted in about 4,400 tariff concessions covering $4.49 billion of trade.

1964-67 – Kennedy Round. For the first time, negotiations departed from product by product approach, to an across the board of linear method of cutting tariffs for industrial goods. The working hypothesis of a 50% target cut in tariff level, was achieved in many areas. Concessions covered an estimated total value of trade of about $40 billion.

1973-79 Tokyo Round – Launched in the Japanese capital, the seventh round resulted in tariff reductions and bindings, covering more than $300 billion of trade. As a result the weighted average tariffs on manufactured goods in the world's nine major industrial markets declined from 7.0% to 4.0%. Agreements were reached on subsidies and counter veiling measures, technical barriers to trade, import licensing procedures, government procurement, customs valuation, a revised anti-dumping code, trade in bovine meat, diary products and civil aircraft.

1986-94 – Uruguay Round – It was the result of the most comprehensive trade negotiations ever undertaken including average tariff cuts of 40% on industrial products, average increase of tariff binding from 21% to 73% for LDCs, from 78% to 99% for developed countries and from 73% to 98% for transitional economies, a comprehensive programme of agricultural reform, phase out of quantitative restrictions on textiles and clothing, new agreements on trade and services, intellectual property rights, sanitary and phytosanitory measures, new sources and trade related investment measures, and strengthened agreements on safeguards, technical barriers, customs valuation, import licensing, state trading subsidies and anti-dumping measures. The Round also strengthened the dispute settlement system and created the WTO.

WTO Agreement

The agreement establishing WTO is called the WTO Agreement. It is the legal instrument through which all countries participating in the Uruguay Round decided to create the WTO. The WTO

Agreement includes provisions on establishment, scope, functions and structure, relations with other organizations, secretariat, budget and contributions, legal status, decision-making procedures, including special voting procedures, amendment, definition of original members, accession, non-application, acceptance, entry into force and deposit mobilisation and final provisions. Since all the other agreements are annexed to the agreement establishing the WTO, the expression **"the WTO Agreement"** is understood to cover the totality of all the agreements. The basic structure of the WTO Agreements is given below:

Umbrella	Agreements	Establishing	WTO
	Goods	Services	Intellectual Property
Basic principles ' Additional details	GATT Other Goods Agreements and Annexes	GATS Services annexes	TRIPS
Market access Commitments	Countries schedule commitments	Countries schedules of commitments (and MFN exceptions)	
Dispute settlement	Dispute settlement		
Transparency	Trade Policy Reviews		

The WTO: Sub-clauses of Agreement

The WTO's agreements are often called the Final Act of the 1986-1994 Uruguay Round of trade negotiations. This is a summary of the Agreements.

1. Agreement on Agriculture (AoA).
2. Agreement on Sanitary and Phytosanitary Measures.
3. Agreement on Textiles and clothing.
4. Agreement on Technical Barriers to Trade (TBT).
5. Agreement on Trade-related Aspects of Investment Measures (TRIMS).
6. Agreement on Implementation of Article VI (Anti-Dumping).

7. Agreement on Implementation of Article VII (Customs Valuation).
8. Agreement on Pre-shipment Inspection (PSI).
9. Agreement on Rules of origin.
10. Agreement on Subsidies and Countervailing Measures.
11. Agreement on Safeguards.
12. General Agreement on Trade in Services.
13. Agreement on Trade Related Aspects of Intellectual Property Rights (TRIPs), including trade in counterfeit goods.

India and the WTO

India is a founding member of the GATT (1947). It actively participated in the Uruguay Round of Negotiations. India strongly favours the multilateral approach to trade relations and grants MFN (Most Favoured Nation) treatment to all its trading partners, including some who are not members of WTO. India has participated actively in all the Ministerial Conferences held under WTO auspicies. India is committed to ensure that the sectors in which the LDCs enjoy a comparative advantage are adequately opened up to international trade, and also that the special and differential treatment provisions for LDCs under the different WTO Agreements are translated into specific enforcable dispensations, in order that LDCs are facilitated in their developmental efforts. India feels that the multilateral system would itself gain if it adequately reflected these concerns of the LDCs, so as to create the necessary impetus to enable developing country members to catch up with their developed country counterparts.

Under the Uruguay Round, India has bound 67% of all its tariff lines, whereas prior to that only 6% of tariff levies were bound. The bindings range from 0% to 300% for agricultural products and from 0% to 40% for other products. Under the Uruguay Round, manufactured products were bound at 25% on intermediate goods, and 40% on finished goods. The phased reduction to these bound levels from the very high levels prevailing in 1990, is where necessary, in installments over the period 1995 to 2005. In Textiles where reductions will be achieved over ten years, India has reserved the right to duty levels prevailing in 1990, if the integration process envisaged under the Agreement on Textiles and Clothing does not materialize in full or is delayed. Finally, in agriculture, except for a few goods, India's bound rates range from100% to 300%. India is in the process of re-negotiating some of its tariff bindings. Many applied tariffs are below the Uruguay Round level.

The forerunner of the European Union (EU) was the EEC (European Economic Community) formed in 1958 with initially six members. Today the EU has 25 members, including some countries of the former Soviet Bloc in Eastern Europe and the newly liberated countries of the former Soviet Union. EU, taken, as a single unit is India's largest trading partner.

India should pay greater attention to the emerging opportunities in the EU, and improve quality of exports and stick to delivery schedules. The accord between the United States, Canada, and Mexico to drop all trade barriers is known as the North America Free Trade Area (NAFTA) accord. The WTO accord was signed in 1995, as part of the conclusion of the Uruguay Round of Trade negotiations. This was a preceded by the GATT (General Agreement on Trade and Tariff) rounds. There were eight rounds of GATT negotiations. India is a founding member of GATT, and as active participant in the Uruguay Round of negotiations. The WTO agreements are thirteen in the number, and called the final act of the Uruguay Round of trade negotiations, which ran from 1986 to 1994.

4

SHORT TERM CAPITAL AND THE EAST ASIAN CRISIS

The Asian Economic Crisis

The Asian financial and economic crisis affected many countries of the ASEAN. This first come to world attention in mid-1997, as the Thai Baht rapidly lost value against the US $. The inter connections among Asian Economies led to its rapid spread to Indonesia, Malaysia, the Philippines, the Republic of Korea and Hong Kong. Many other countries in the region, such as Vietnam, Japan, Australia and Singapore, were also adversely affected.

Indonesia was the worst affected by this economic crisis. According to the Asian Development Bank (ADB), the GDP of Indonesia was estimated to have contracted by 1.32% in 1998. In 1999, however the country's GDP increased by 0.9% in 2000, by 4.8% and in 2001 by 3.3%. By 1999, the regions economies all began to recover. In 2000, ADB estimates placed Singapore and Malaysia at growth rates of 9.9 per cent and 8.5 per cent respectively, while the economy of Thailand expanded by 0.2% and that of the Philippines by 3.9 per cent. In 2001, however, owing to the global economic downturn (particularly in the electronics sector) Singapore's GDP contracted by 2%.

The predatory role played by currency speculators, and the extent of damage inflicted throughout the ASEAN region via the contagion effect, aggravated the financial crisis. There is certainly need to subject currency trading to some sort of surveillance, transparency, accountability and discipline, as the value of currencies traded far exceeds that of trade in goods and services across the globe. Heavy industries, including automotive and iron and steel were inefficient and under heavy protection. Unsound banking practices and poor corporate governance also contributed significantly to the financial turmoil. Massive outflow of capital in the form of "reserve investments" to finance long-term projects, with no prospects of early harvests exacerbated Balance of Payments (BoP) problems.

The unpredictable nature of the crisis is certainly a cause for concern. In particular, the self-fulfilling nature of financial market expectations, chain reactions and herd behaviour led to massive capital movements in a manner that is remotely connected to the fundamentals. All these have made highflying ASEAN economies particularly vulnerable. While the crisis was clearly trigged by external forces, poor governance at home must share the blame to the extent, that it has contributed to the vulnerability of these economies to external shocks. Sound prudential and banking norms, less gung-ho and Crony capitalism, and good corporate governance have put the ASEAN economies on the recovery track.

International Trade, Financial Flows and the LDCs

In international capital markets, there has been an increase in risk premiums and less willingness by investors to lend to LDCs at a time when their external financing needs to meet rising current account deficits have been growing.

The LDCs did not benefit from inflows of capital seeking alternative destinations or higher returns as the prospects for profits in financial markets in industrial countries deteriorated. The lower incomes due to the slow down in exports and falling petroleum prices reduced fiscal receipts for many LDCs, and by cutting expenditures to keep their budgets in balance they further aggravated the down turn in economic activity. Finally, substantial declines in inflation rates and, indeed, the absolute level of consumer prices, in a large number of developed countries, tended to limit corporate profitability and reduced the likelihood of a return to high investment rates.

Financial Markets and Capital Flows

Capital flows to LDCs in 2001 remained at low levels, prolonging the downward trend that persisted since the 1997 Asian financial crisis. In 2001 South America was the largest recipient of inflows, despite a substantial decline in inflows to Argentina. Other regions, with the exception of West Asia and Turkey, also received positive inflows.

The interest rate reduction in the early 1990s, following a decade of historically high rates in the US, induced many investors to shift their investments to emerging LDC markets in order to maintain high returns. The attraction of these investments was supported by the rapid rates of economic expansion in Asia, and the apparent success of adjustment policies in Argentina and Mexico in the early 1990s, and in Brazil in 1994. Liberalization of financial markets in these countries, also increased their attractiveness as investment alternatives. As a result of increased global economic integration, and the greater role of external trade in the economies of LDCs, the downturn of the US had a more rapid negative impact on their growth and export performance than in the past.

In many Asian countries recovering from the 1997 crisis, large external surpluses have been a source of increased deposits with international banks. Since 1998, repayments to banks by borrowers in all LDCs have exceeded new loans to them, and the total exposure of BIS (Bank for International Settlements) – reporting banks to such economies is now more than $200 billion, lower than in 1997. Net repayments to BIS-reporting banks by borrowers in East and South Asia, and in oil exporting countries in West Asia have been accompanied by a large build up of deposits by the two regions, which reflects substantial current account surpluses. There has been a substantial net source of funds to the international banking system.

Financing for LDCs in the form of export credit also declined in later years. Estimates of net capital flows to LDCs, and transition economies from 1998 to 2002 in billions of dollars are shown in the table 1 below:

The Main Causes of the South East Asian Economic Crisis

The principal reasons for the South East Asian crisis existing in Thailand in mid-1997 and spreading to Malaysia, Indonesia, Philippines and South Korea were

Table 1

Estimates of Net Capita Flows to Developing and Transition Economies, 1998-2002

(Billions of $) Estimates of IMF

Type of flow / region	*1998*	*1999*	*2000*	*2001*	*2002*
TOTAL	69.6	59.6	8.9	20.1	59.8
Net direct investment	155.4	153.4	146.2	162.4	142.6
Net portfolio investment	-4.2	31.0	-4.3	-13.0	13.7
Other net flows	-81.6	-124.8	-133.0	-129.4	-96.6
AFRICA	10.0	11.9	7.0	9.5	10.0
Net direct investment	6.9	9.0	7.2	21.4	11.0
Net portfolio investment	3.7	8.7	-1.8	-6.3	4.2
Other net flows	-0.7	-5.8	1.6	-5.8	-5.2
ASIA	-53.4	-7.6	-12.2	1.4	-3.1
Net direct investment	59.9	51.9	46.8	43.7	41.7
Net portfolio investment	-15.3	13.8	3.7	-4.7	3.8
Other net flows	-89.4	-74.4	-66.4	-46.0	-50.1
MIDDLE EAST AND EUROPE	11.8	-1.1	-22.4	-29.2	-0.7
Net direct investment	6.3	5.4	7.2	6.5	8.4
Net portfolio investment	-13.2	-4.2	-15.1	-9.6	-5.2
Other net flows	8.6	-2.3	-14.6	-26.1	-3.8
WESTERN HEMISPHERE	71.7	43.6	37.9	38.8	39.5
Net direct investment	60.7	63.8	62.5	64.1	50.0
Net portfolio investment	16.5	9.8	4.6	4.0	7.6
Other net flows	-5.5	-30.0	-29.2	-29.3	-18.0
TRANSITION ECONOMIES	21.0	13.8	2.2	7.6	15.0
Net direct investment	21.6	23.4	22.5	26.7	31.5
Net portfolio investment	4.0	2.8	4.3	3.6	3.5
Other net flows	-4.6	-12.4	-24.7	-22.7	-20.0

Source: IMF, World Economic Outlook (December 2001)

1. Large current account deficits.
2. Unmanagable foreign debt, particularly a high proportion of short term debt.
3. Uncontrolled inflows of foreign capital, particularly sensitive short term capital.
4. Indiscriminate lending by banks and other financial institutions, arising from lack of adherence to sound prudential norms concerning capital adequacy, asset classification, provisioning, and sound disclosure guidelines.
5. Lack of transparency in the economic system that makes proper judgment by investors difficult.
6. Over-investment in many crucial areas.
7. Improper lending by international lending institutions.
8. Real effective exchange rate appreciation.

The crisis first occurred in Thailand. The cheap Thai labour attracted a lot of FDI from Japan, and other neighbouring countries. Large portfolio investments and short term funds started pouring into Thailand. The South East Asian countries had fixed exchange rates, which attracted more foreign capital. Banks also indiscriminately lent to Thailand, resulting in the over-expansion of several industries. There was also speculative investment in real estate, which lead to occupancy rates of buildings reaching an all time law. The increased demand for labour made Thai labour, very costly- five times more costly than the labour in neighbouring countries. Thai exports suffered set backs due to increasing costs, and the high costs led to huge imports, causing serious current account deficits. The impression gained that the Thai Baht would be devalued shortly. There was thus a run on the Baht – people desperately wanted to convert the Baht into dollars, so that they could re exchange dollars for more units of Baht, when it would be devalued. The Thai Central Bank sold billions of dollars in forward movements, in a desperate attempt to defend the Baht. This led to unabashed speculation. Finally, the Baht was allowed to proof. It immediately depreciated by initially 20% and much further after some time. The crisis led to short term foreign investors withdrawing their money. The crisis rapidly spread to other South East Asian countries, where conditions were similar or worse than Thailand. Depreciation of countries across South East Asia (except Singapore) and including South Korea was rapid. As the South East Asian countries were highly integrated with the rest of the world, the crisis had global ramifications. The extremely high foreign trade to GDP ratio of these nations, led to the accentuation of the crisis, as were inward outward capital flows.

India and the South East Asian Crisis

The south East Asian crisis largely left India untouched. The current account deficit of India was within managable limits. The foreign debt ratios have shown improvement over the years, and the proportion of short term list was comparatively very low in 1997. The financial sector is well regulated, and the NPAs (Non-performing Assets) of banks within managable limits. It may be noted that, volatile FII (Foreign Institutional Investment) flows and short term debt are major areas of concern, and are a substantial amount of India's investment profile. This, as has happened recently, can destabalise the positive aspect, of India's macro-economic picture.

The South East Asian melt down and recession did have a moderate impact of India's exports. South East Asia accounted for about 1/10th of India's foreign trade, and several domestic industries also came under strain, because of cheap imports from these economies.

A major aspect of the South East crisis was felt on investment flows. The fall in asset prices, encouraged Indian investment in South East Asia. Apart from economic distortions, the political instability and internal disturbances adversely affected investment sentiment in India. However, the turn around in South East Asian economies was equally rapid, and they bounced back to moderate growth rates fairly rapidly.

5

IMF (INTERNATIONAL MONETARY FUND), IBRD (INTERNATIONAL BANK FOR RECONSTRUCTION AND DEVELOPMENT, ADB (ASIAN DEVELOPMENT BANK)

The UNCTAD or the United Nations Conference on Trade and Development was formed in 1964, as a permanent organ of the United Nations. It was formed because of the general dissatisfaction of the LDCs with IMF and GATT, and the need for new international economic cooperation in the field of trade and aid. The Conference, is a plenary body of a large member of countries, and meets every four years. It has a perman7ent organ, the Trade and Development Board, the main executive body functioning between plenary sessions of the Conference for an effective discharge of functions. The Board has four subsidiary organizations or committees on (*i*) Commodities (*ii*) Manufactures (*iii*) Shipping and (*iv*) Invisibles and Financing related to trade. The major recommendations of the conference of UNCTAD are:

1. There should be agreed criteria for disposal of surplus stocks of all primary products, and they should be disposed of in such a way as to promote economic development of all LDCs, whether as producers or recipients of such surplus products.

2. Developed countries should grant unilateral tariff reductions or preferences to the LDCs. Such tariff reductions on the part of developed countries, will increase the exports of LDCs, and will lead to an increase in imports from developed countries, and expansions of international trade.

3. International loans to LDCs on conessional terms should increase substantially.
4. The visible trade of LDCs should go up.
5. Price stabilization measures should be adopted on an equitable and universal basis, without prejudices to the financial aid to LDCs.
6. Developed countries and international financial institutions, should take steps to develop communication facilities to overcome problems of land locked countries.
7. The LDCs should achieve better trade cooperation and regional economic integration among themselves.

The effectiveness of UNCTAD as an institution to protect third world interest declined in recent years, with the advent of globalization.

International Monetary Fund (IMF)

The IMF is an organization of countries that seeks to promote international monetary cooperation, and to facilitate the expansion of trade, and thus to contribute to increased employment and improved economic conditions in all member countries. The member countries of the fund today account for over 90 per cent of world production, and 95 per cent of world trade. A close working relationship exists between the IMF and the World Bank and they function more-or-less in tandem. WTO, and the BIS (Bank of International Settlements) at Basel, Switzerland, also work in close coordination with IMF.

Functions of the IMF

The main functions of the IMF are :

1. To promote international monetary cooperation through a permanent institution, which provides the machinery for consultation and collaboration on international monetary problems.
2. To facilitate the expansion and balanced growth of international trade and to contribute thereby to the promotion

and maintenance of high levels of employment and real income, and to the development of the productive resources of all members, as primary objectives of economic policy.

3. To promote exchange stability, to maintain orderly exchange arrangements among members, and to avoid competitive exchange depreciations.
4. To eliminate foreign exchange restrictions, which hamper the growth of world trade.
5. To give confidence to members for making general resources of the Fund temporarily available to them under adequate safeguards, thus providing them with an opportunity to correct functions in their BoPs.
6. In accordance with the above five guidelines, to shorten the duration and less the degree of disequilibrium in the international BoPs.

The IMF thus combines three major functions : (*a*) Regulatory (*b*) Financial and (*c*) Consultative.

To achieve its purposes, the Fund has a code of economic behaviour for its members – Member countries of the IMF undertake to collaborate with the Fund and with other countries to assure orderly exchange arrangements, and a stable system of exchange rates, together with a multilateral system of payments among countries. Members are free to choose the from of exchange arrangements they intend to apply, subject to their obligations to the fund, and it its surveillance of their exchange rate policies.

The IMF maintains a large pool of financial resources that it makes applicable to member countries temporarily and subject to conditions to enable them to carry out programmes to remedy their payments deficits, without resorting to restrictive measures that could adversely affect national and international progress. The IMF member - countries coordinate internationally their economic policies. Thus, there is ongoing process of international monetary reform and adjustment.

The resources of the IMF come from two sources—(*i*) subscription by members and (*ii*) borrowings.

Every member of the IMF is required to subscribe to the Fund an amount equivalent to its quota. The Quota system is central to the IMF. The members are assigned quotas expressed in SDRs (Special Drawing Rights). A member's SDR contribution determines the voting power, reflecting economic size in relationship to total membership of the Fund. The IMF is authorized, under its Articles of Agreement to supplement its ordinary resources by borrowings. Under the GAB (General Agreement to Borrow) important (with economic potential) countries of the developed world have decided to lend to the IMF to prevent any disruption of the international monetary system.

World Bank (IBRD)

The World Bank or International Bank for Reconstruction and Development (IBRD), the other twin of IMF – together they are known as Bretton – Woods Twins – was established in 1945 . The IBRD has two affiliates – the IDA (International Development Association) established in 1960, and the IFC (International Finance Corporation), established in 1956.

The IBRD is owned by the government of member countries. The IBRD, capital being member – subscribed, finances its lending operations, primarily from its own borrowings, in the world's capital markets. Under the Articles of Agreement of the Bank, all powers are vested with the Bank's Board of Governors, on which each member country is represented by one Governor. The Governors of the Bank have delegated their powers to a Board of Executive Directors, which perform their duties on a full time basis at the Banks Head Quarters. There are 21 Executive Directors, who are appointed by the five members, having the largest number of shares of capital stock, and the rest are elected by Governors, representing the other member countries.

The World Bank, which traditionally financed all kinds of capital infrastructure such as roads, railways, telecommunications, port, and power facilities, changed its development strategy, with the emphasis on investments directly affecting the well-being of the masses, and integrating them as active partners in the development process. In recent years, the IBRD has stepped up, its lending for energy development - power reforms form the largest part of the Banks energy programme. Commitments have been made towards oil and gas development.

In 1980 the Bank introduced the SAL (Structural Adjustment Lending). This lending supports programmes of specific policy changes and international reforms in LDCs to achieve more efficient use of resources. In 1983, a SAP (Special Action Programme) designed to increase assistance to countries making efforts with the exceptionally difficult geo-economic environment, was instituted.

In future lending strategies, the IBRD will continue to be concerned with the distributional aspects of economic growth. The World Bank (IBRD) must restructure its operations to complement, its developmental role in LDCs.

The Asian Development Bank (ADB)

The ADB was set up in 1966, under the auspicious of the UN ESCAP (Economic and Social Commission for Asia and Pacific) to foster economic development, particularly for Asian countries. Its Head Quarters are in Manila, the Philippines.

The ADB's core strategy is combating poverty through infrastructure – led growth, public – private partnership and labour market strategies for inclusive growth and susitainable energy development in Asia. ADB has projected that the Asia – Pacific region will achieve overall expansion of 7.2% in 2006, and 8% by 2007.

India, a founding member of the ADB, started borrowing from the Bank since 1986. It has borrowed loans uptp $14 billion till 2005. As per its latest India "Country Strategy and Progress" – update, ADB plans to scale-up lending levels to India.

However, the "development model" of ADB is being questioned, and the efficiency of projects being promoted by the Bank raises questions of transparency, corruption, and accountability. South Asian countries feel that the agenda of ADB is profiteering, and promotion of free-market based capitalist economy at the cost of public sector, built by public money in the LDCs. Asian countries feel that ADB promotes "indefinite poverty" in the name of development.

6

PROBLEMS OF INTERNATIONAL DEBT-INDIAN AND INTERNATIONAL

Background of India's External Debt

In 1998, for the first time an "International Working Group" defined external debt to include amount of disbursed and outstanding liabilities of the residents of a country to non-residents, to repay principal with or without interest.

In 1991, the Government of India for the first time felt the need to establish policy groups to review the existing system of classification of India's external debt. The Report released by the RBI in 1992, was to ensure uniformity and transparency in India's external debt management.

Classification of External Debt

The eight categories of external debt by type of credit are Debt to: (*i*) Multinationals, (*ii*) Bilateral Debt, (*iii*) IMF (International Monetary Fund) outstandings, (*iv*) Commercial borrowings, (*v*) Non-Resident Deposits, (*vi*) Non-Resident Bonds, (*vii*) Short Term Debt including NRI (Non-Resident Indian) Deposits up to one year, and (*viii*) Export Credits.

India's External Debt as Percentage of GDP

India external debt as a percentage of GDP was 36.9 per cent in 1993-94. This is comparable with Thailand and Malaysia, and is much lower than the figures for Indonesia, Philippines and Turkey. The debt service payments over various years are given in the table below:

Table 2

Projected Debt Service Payments

(In U.S. $ million)

Year	*Principal*	*Interest*	*Total*
1999-2000	6527	2816	9140
2000-2001	6202	2512	8723
2001-2002	5910	2165	8075
2002-2003	6301	1895	8196
2003-2004	9512	2843	12555

Source: Ministry of Finance, India's External Debt – A Status Report.

Causes and Consequences of India's Debt Crisis

In the recent past, the Indian economy depended more on direct foreign investment and such other forms of long term capital inflows to insulate itself from external shocks.

The first cause of our debt crisis is the gap between imports and exports, greatly aggravated over the past decade.

Another cause of the crisis is that even as the trade deficit burgeoned, we were increasingly sensible to service these out of current receipts from invisible items such as tourism, and workers remittances.

An important cause for the shortfall in net receipts from invisibles was the mounting debt burden of interest payments on India's mounting external debts.

The debt crisis in the 90s looked increasingly like a debt trap. The substantiality of the debt burden depends to a large extent on the terms of borrowings rather than on the level of debt or GNP ratio. The debt of many LDCs, particularly in sub-Saharan Africa has reached more than 60% of their GNP.

Debt Crisis in India – Latest Trends

In India, despite increasing debt stock in recent years, there has been a substantial improvement, in external debt indicators. Debt service ratio declined from the peak of 35.5% in 1990-91 to 15.4% in 2001, and further to 13% in 2002-03. This implies that the country could meet its debt service obligations by less than one-seventh of the current receipts. The debt to GDP ratio, which signifies the extent of external debt in relation to domestic output declined from 40% in 1991-92 to 21% in 2002-03.

From 1991 to 2002-03, short-term debt to total debt ratio declined form 10.2% to 2.8%, short-term debt to GDP ratio from 3% to 0.6% and short-term debt to foreign exchange assets ratio from a high of 58.2% to 6.1%. Among the top 15 debtor countries of the world, India improved its rank from the largest debtor after Brazil and Mexico in 1991, to the ninth position in 2000 after Brazil, Russia, Mexico, China, Argentina, Indonesia, Korea and Turkey.

In terms of indebtedness classification, the World Bank, has categorized India as a less indebted country since 1999, whereas it was in the severely indebted category in1991, and envisaged as a moderately indebted country till 1998.

If we compare India with other LDCs, India has relied less on external aid, and after the Third Five Year Plan, our reliance on foreign funds has been marginal.

The per capita external debt in India is, therefore small by LDC standards. But, the burden of external debt on people can be measured in relation to current earnings.

In recent years, the RBI and Ministry of Finance have taken a number of pro-active measures to check high interest debts and moderated interest rates.

However, economic reforms should focus on mitigating the harsh consequences of the burden of debt, particularly among the economically disadvantaged sections.

International Debt Problem

The external debt of the LDCs threatened to engulf the creditors, mainly developed countries, once Mexico, Brazil and Argentina were affected by the crisis in the early 1980s.

External debt ratios are high for a number of countries. Debt servicing, that is, repaying back debt of LDCs, aggregates the problems of LDCs.

There are many reasons for the debt problems of LDCs. There have been two oil shocks in the 1970s – 1973-74 and 1979. This aggravated debt problems. The financing arrangements caused by the huge deficits of LDCs, were such that the resources of the IMF were not sufficient to pay back their debts. Commercial borrowing was resorted to by some LDCs, and the international banking system recycled the surplus of oil exporters into loans for importers. However interest rates at which commercial borrowers had to repay was very high.

The external debt also has a lot to do with the management of the domestic economy and economic policies of LDCs. Political stability and economic stability affect capital flows. Efficient utilization of international institutions funds also does not take place. IMF Report have clearly shown that domestic and external debt are closely linked in many countries. The Latin American debt crisis, leading to large scale LDC default, threatened the poor world's stability and the rich world's banking system. Third world liquidity became a problem of solvency. Thus "debt traps" emerged rapidly. Nine US banks were becoming bankrupt, if three Latin American countries – Argentina, Brazil and Mexico defaulted on foreign debt. The US Treasury Secretary, James Baker announced a plan for growth – oriented economic reforms in debtor countries. The World Bank was brought into the fray along with the IMF for the "Baker plan". However, the Baker plan was only for the Western Hampshire countries, and it has been alleged that it was more of a vested interest scheme than a general plan. It thus had only a limited impact. Debt write-off got the official stamp in the meeting of Group of Seven in Toronto. Nine industrial countries in the OECD announced plans to help low-income African countries, either by write-off of bilateral loans or converting loans into grants. The new US Treasury Secretary, Nicholas Bradley agreed to debt write-off following proposals by France and Japan. Many proposals also emerged from commonwealth

Finance Ministers meets, meeting of ministers from LDCs (South) and other for a. Both donors are to blame, as well as LDCs for inconsistent economic policies. However, despite many inconsistencies of both donors and LDCs, debt burden was eased and the world heaved a sigh of relief. The sub-saharan African countries however, did not recover fully because of their own mis-management of their countries. External debt made a contribution to some extent to the South East Asian economic crisis of the late 1990s.

7

MNCS (MULTI-NATIONAL CORPORATIONS) IN INDIA

Definition of an MNC

An MNC owns and controls income generation assets in more than one country, and in doing so produces goods and services outside its country of origin. Its managerial headquarters are located in the country referred to as the "home country", while the enterprise carries out operations in a number of countries, known as host countries. Thus, it has the character of giant size, international operations, oligopolistic structure, spontaneous evaluation and collective transfer of resources. MNCs are also referred to as TNCs (Trans National Corporations), which implies that their operations extend beyond the boundaries of a nation in which they are originally envisaged.

MNCs in India – Background

India started planning her economy in 1951, with a blend of public and private sectors. It was a so-called "mixed economy". In the 1960s, India became a more or less closed economy, raising tariff walls. Our export-orientation was very limited, and we were very suspicious of foreign investment, and foreign capital, despite facing a domestic resource crunch. Our technology was also outdated, and economy protected and industrial licensing policy, working against rapid industrialization. In the 1970s, our BOP (Balance of Payments) became distorted, and we had to borrow a massive loan of 2.5 billion dollars from the IMF. The MNCs are increasing their hold over the Indian economy since the 1970s, and today control about 53 per cent of the assets of the industrial sector in India. The growth of MNCs through collaboration with Indian industries has been fast during the 1980s. In the 1980s with the coming to power of Rajiv Gandhi, liberalization and deregulation started gaining momentum but gathered full pace only in the 1990s, with the coming to power of Dr. Manmohan singh as Finance Minister and P.V. Narasimha Rao as Prime Minister in 1991. They initiated a process of liberalization, privatization and globalization and transformed the Indian economy, making it vibrant and competitive.

Impact of MNCs on various sectors of the Indian Economy

The impact of MNCs on industrial development of India during the 1980s reveals that during the period 1990-92, the index of industrial production increased from 47.6% in 1970, to 155.8% in 1992. The contribution of manufacturing sector to industrial development increased considerably. The Industrial Policy of 1991 contributed significantly to the rise of MNCs in the Indian economy. The main features of the Industrial Policy of 1991 are:

(*i*) To accelerate the pace of industrial growth, by providing greater freedom in investment decisions, keeping in view the objectives of increasing exports, efficiency and competitiveness of the industry. The policy encourages foreign investment, and provides enhanced access to state-of-the art technology, to enable advances in production techniques, and helps in the attainment of international competitiveness.

(*ii*) Industrial licensing has been abolished for all industries, except for six reserved for the public sector, those reserved for the small sector, and 15 industries that have compulsory licensing.

(*iii*) In order to attract foreign investment in high priority industries, involving large investments and advanced technologies, direct investment upto 51% foreign equity is being freely permitted.

(*iv*) A system of informatic approvals has been introduced for speedy clearance of proposals.

(*v*) Foreign brand names and trade marks of goods is also freely permitted.

As a consequence of the 1991 industrial policy, the FDI approvals in India dramatically increased. However, despite best efforts by the government, FDI flows average only about 5 billion dollars a year, compared to annual flows of 30 billion dollars to China.

Effect on Capital Movement

International Capital flows help people to achieve a smoother consumption profile. Welfare would be greater with cross-border capital flows. The most important vehicle for cross border capital flows have been FDI (Foreign Direct Investment). With the emergence of MNCs, production and distribution of goods and services has been globalised during the last four decades.

The political and economic power that MNCs possess at times, is to the disadvantage of host countries. A regime of MNCs would offer LDCs neither national independence nor equality. It would tend to inhibit the attainment of these goals. The LDCs would be reduced to branches of the host country. MNCs, not only with reference to economic functions, but throughout the whole gamut of social, political and cultural roles would be subservient to the interests of outside big powers with only economic muscle power.

Country, referred to as the 'home country' while the enterprise carries out operations in a number of countries, known as host countries.

The industrial policy of 1991 contributed significantly to the rise of MNCs in the Indian economy.

The political and economic power that MNCs possess at times is to the disadvantages of host countries.

MNCs add a tremendous amount of managerial know how and international exposure. In the world of globalization and market integration, the role of MNCs are likely to expand further. Host country governments need to reframe that lows, to maximize return from MNC investments.

8

REVISITING REFORMS AND GLOBALIZATION IN INDIA

1.1 Globalization-background

Global ization gained momentum from the mid-1980s. The global ization of markets and marketization of economics, politics and culture was spearheaded by global capitalism. In terms of politics and international relations, globalization means a greater bonding or coming together of nation states. With the collapse of communism, end of the cold war, integration into EU and NATO of former East-bloc countries, together with the fading away of non-aligned and of the North-South conflict, nations are moving closer to each other, like never before.

Greater internationalization, globalization and integration seem to be the new order of the day. Regional integration is taking place all over the world. In Europe, the EEC or the European Economic Community has given place to the EU or European Union, where the now twenty-five members have made further efforts at monetary and financial integration with the ultimate goal of full political union. In Asia greater steps towards regional integration have resulted in the formation of AFTA (ASEAN Free Trade Area), a re-vitalised SAARC (South Asian Association for Regional Co-operation) with a determination to form a SAFTA (South Asian Free Trade Area) and B1MSTEC (Bay of Bengal Initiative for Multi-Sectoral Technical and Economic Co-operation) (Bangladesh, India, Myanmar, Sri Eanka, Thailand with Nepal and Bhutan also joining); while new Pan-Regional organizations like APEC (Asia Pacific Economic Community) and the SCO (Shanghai Co-operation Organizations) have emerged. In North America, the US, Mexico and Canada joined to form NAFTA (North American Free Trade Area) while in Africa a newly democratized South Africa has joined its former front-line enemies in Southern Africa to revitalize the newly named SADC (Southern African Development Community).

Thus in international relations, globalization has meant nations shedding their ideological and political differences and forming new alliances, and trading groups and increasingly cooperating in international fora like the UN and in other world bodies like the IMF, the World Bank and WTO (World Trade Organisation).

Globalization in socio-cultural terms means opening up our society to influences, cultures and patterns of behaviour of other nations and trying to spread our culture and influence to others. In reality, LDCs and nascent modernizing societies like India are more prone to be influenced by external cultural influences than to export their own culture and value systems. This is because the media play a major role in the "globalization" or "internationalization" process. Now the print media from abroad certainly have a strong influence on our urban elites; but much more pervasive is the influence of the visual and electronic media: and in a traditional and largely conservative society like India, the visual impact of foreign life styles can be psychologically un-nerving. The open-skies policy of the government of India allowing foreign electronic media via satellites to penetrate Indian homes surely has a powerful influence on the social fabric of the nation, which can be strained if rural India develops unfulfillable aspirations for the consumption patterns of foreign societies. Globalisation encourages consumerism and speculation-more is less in a globalised world. On the other hand, the growing demand from rural India may lead to un-fulfilled expectations.

The positive feature is the adaptive-response time may be reduced owing to better telecommunication facilities, so that in areas like medicine, science and technology and the latest trends in informatics, Indian society may well leapfrog into the future. In economic terms, "Globalization" means developing an outward market orientation rather than the inward looking policy of depending solely on domestic markets. Economic globalization means opening our doors and windows to goods, services and investment from other countries of the world, while trying to export our own goods and services to the outside world.

India's Autarkic Past

Independent India entertained autarkic notions of eliminating external influences and tried to cut itself from the global economy instead of seeking opportunities in it. As a result, India's share of world trade fell from 2.5% in 1947 to 0.7% today because of a conscious decision to de-emphasize foreign trade, the free flow of technology and foreign investment. India also got bogged down in the notion that aid and not trade was the stuff of 'which development was made. It failed to recognize that dynamic businessmen not clever bureaucrats would transform a backward economy. Until recently our response to the global economy has been reactive and negative. Our national economy has stayed on the fringes of the world. We participated in international trade only at the minimum, unavoidable levels, importing only what was absolutely needed and could not be produced domestically and exporting just enough to pay for these imports. Over the decades the Indian economy operated in a planned set up, within a framework of regulations and controls, with the public sector occupying the "commanding heights". On the other hand, the successful developing countries of Asia struck out another path. They first developed their human capital through insistence on universal education and public health, fields in which India has done badly. Secondly, they recognized that entrepreneurial energies of their businessmen were a prime asset and encouraged them to launch forth, while we equated profit with sin. Thirdly they created an economic system where innovation and productivity yielded the most profit, not licence manipulation. Fourthly, they ensured that commercial principles ruled in the supply of basic services like power, transport and finance. We on the other hand have indulged in politically motivated giveaways, which destroy the very institutions concerned. Fifthly, they made sure that production for export was at least as profitable as production for domestic consumption, thus giving international trade a key role in development. Until the end of the 1970s,India's trade policy was basically guided by import substitution. A trade regime with high protective walls and import quotas afforded open-ended protection to domestic import-competing industries with no comparable encouragement to exports. This created a high cost, low quality and high profit domestic economy. Entrepreneurs were stripped of the very desire to export, apart from being unable to do so, owing to the high cost and low quality of their products. Exports had, therefore, to be provided with many concessions like duty free imports, duty drawbacks, exemptions, from income tax and cash compensatory support. On the other hand, considerable progress was achieved in diversifying the economy through a continuous planning process with slow improvement in the GDP growth rate. Finally, in the eighties a tendency developed towards relaxation of the crippling regulatory system, in response to dynamic changes and growing pressures, both domestic and global. However, these moves towards deregulation, liberalization and opening up of the economy initiated in the and early'SOs were piecemeal, not systematic, and not integrated into any overall policy framework. India's arms-length relationship with the global economy could not however continue indefinitely. In June 1991,the country awoke to the dire consequences of its closed, regulated economy. In was hit by a balance of payments crisis, being left with a foreign exchange reserves of just $1 billion, enough for 15 days of essential imports. The country was on the verge of bankruptcy and default on its foreign debts. Simultaneously there was a decline in foreign aid. Hence, there was a desperate need to accelerate growth to seek foreign markets for our goods and services and to explore ways of attracting foreign capital and technology. In other words, India's own urgent needs required links with the rest of the world. Simultaneously the world outside had radically changed. Today, a large volume of economic and financial transactions takes place outside the network of government agencies. This has reduced the role of central banks like the Reserve Bank of India (RBI) and increased the role of MNCs (Multi National Companies). A sizable volume of financial transfers across national frontiers today constitutes the internal accounts of MNCs in which they alone take key decisions. Revolutionary changes in transport and communication systems, liberalized trading arrangements, the relaxation of foreign exchange controls in most industrialised countries and many NIC's (newly industrializing countries) and the diffusion of new technology had dramatically increased the degree of interdependence among nations, leading to an unprecedented increase in international trade in goods and services and in the volume of capital and technology flows, benefiting the participating countries enormously- the same time, this interdependence has reduced the area over which domestic policy used to exercise sole control. In other words, the individual countries have become more amenable or rather more vulnerable to external influences. Even the most powerful economies find that there are limits to governmental action. India is obviously even more vulnerable. Clearly, national interest demanded that we accept the world as it is and looked for opportunities to strengthen our economy and gradually outgrow the league of minor players. Any other course would have been suicidal. Now, greater participation in the global economy means that we have to learn the rules of the game of globalization and how to use them to our advantage.

Preamble to the New Economic Policy

Trade policies had been somewhat liberalized during the 1980s and three long term export-import (EXIM) policies had been announced by the government-the first in 1985,the second in 1988 and the third in 1990.Import licensing was considerably liberalized to provide domestic producers access to cheaper capital goods, intermediates and raw materials and to help them upgrade technology. A number of items were placed in the OGL (Open General Licence) list and required no import licence.since July 1991,however, policies have moved consistently towards deregulation, liberalization and globalization of the economy on an irreversible basis. The major changes in policy fall under five heads-Industrial, Trade, Financial, Fiscal and Monetary.We will concentrate on the trade policy reforms, since these are crucial in the globalization efforts of India.The new government first undertook a comprehensive review of the existing export and import policy, and announced major structural trade reforms on July 4,1991 and subsequently on August 13,the same year. These reforms aimed at vigorous elimination or reduction of import licensing, encouragement to exports and promotion of savings. The main features of this policy were as follows: A new EXIM Scrip system enabling easier imports.

1. The grant of additional licences to manufacture.

2. Decanalisation of imports and exports enabling private parties to enter.

3. Abolition of Cash Compensatory Support (CCS) for exports. On March 31,1992 the Commerce Ministry announced a stable liberalized export-import policy for the next five years (1992-1997). Trade would be free, subject to only a small negative list of exports. The basic aim was to strengthen liberalisation policies and to make trade policies simple, transparent and easy to administer. The negative list of imports is the smallest ever; three items were banned, 68 items restricted and only eight items canalised through public sector trading houses. The negative list of exports was pruned with only seven items banned 62 items subject to restrictions and 10 items canalised. Import of capital goods was liberalized and no longer remained on the negative list. EPCG (Export Promotion of Capital Goods) scheme was liberalized and extended to components of capital goods with a concessional customs duty of 15%. Imports of raw materials were also liberalised and barring a few items, raw materials no longer appear in the negative list. The definition of 'deemed exports' was clarified. The following three kinds of organisations are now eligible for special import licences- (a) Export Houses, (b) Trading Houses, (c) Manufactures with ISO 9000 or BIS 14000 certification. A national campaign for quality awareness was to be launched and laboratories and testing houses were to be upgraded and accredited. Concurrent policy reforms were made with regard to Industrial Policy; the Public Sector; Factor Markets, including labour, capital and the financial sector; Tariff policy and the 'Administered Price' policy. The structural reforms in the spheres of trade, industry, finance and the public sector were expected to impart dynamism and efficiency to the growth process and to provide a solid foundation for industrial revival and for acceleration of India's globalisation efforts.

Aspects of Economic Globalizaton

1. *Foreign Trade And Investment*

Our global trade pattern since 1991 is more or less in consonance with political and economic developments the world over. Exports to GCA (general currency areas) have increased. With the collapse of the Soviet Union and the growing turmoil in the newly liberated economies of Eastern Europe, both our exports and imports to and from this region have drastically declined. As a result foreign trade in Rupee terms has virtually disappeared. One favourable aspect of this development is that we now earn more hard currencies. Besides we have been obliged to improve the quality of our products greatly.

While we should strengthen our position in the US and Western Europe, it is now high time for Indian business to fan out to new regions of the world. In SouthEast Asia, Malaysia is becoming saturated with Indian ventures and hence we should make further inroads into Thailand, Singapore and the Indo-Chinese countries. In Africa, the Francophone West African countries have been almost ignored; though there does exist scope for an Indian commercial presence. South America and the Caribbean countries can also be explored for Indian expertise and manegerial contributions particularly in regard to small-scale industries. Similarly there are good prospects once Russia opens up Siberia for international ventures. Eastern Europe offers immense possibilities for our private sector companies to establish production-sharing arrangements.

The government of India has identified 34 export thrust areas where Indian products should do well, such as marine products, horticulture, floriculture, jewellery, bicycles and granite. Export units in these areas are being provided infrastructural support and development assistance to increase their existing strengths. It is important to concentrate on a few products where we have a competitive advantage rather than try to make market inroads with an amorphous group of products. It has to be kept in mind that in the new EU (European Union) there will be an increasing demand for "branded goods" with appeal to specific categories of consumers. At the same time, customers around the world will look for products with special fashion appeal. Thus "niche marketing" will become increasingly important. In our view India has the potential to carve out exclusive "niches" for itself in leather garments for up-market consumers in Europe and in designer cotton wear for the younger generation in the US and Western Europe.Food processing and computer software are also areas which hold a lot of promise for India's overseas business forays.

2. Right Selection of Personnel

Besides, the product profile and country spectrum, an important aspect in globalisation efforts is manpower training. The selection of personnel to go abroad should be very carefully done. Only the best managers who have worked competently in various functional areas at home should be sent abroad. The mindset of people sent abroad should be such that they are equally competent to work in an alien milieu. Thus a common complaint among Japanese and South Korean business undertakings is that Indian businessmen are overbearing in their dealings and have a supercilious attitude. It has to be realised that while keeping pace with the West may be important, the grace of the East has to be given due consideration if we want to succeed in East Asia.This requires proper orientation and cross-cultural training prior to an overseas assignment. The manager working abroad has to deal with people with different value systems, inter-personal behaviour patterns and work practices. He has to interact with such business associates in a culturally appropriate manner. This calls for adequate orientation and training in languages, legal procedures, and customs and above all in suitable reactions and responses so that the sensitivities of the host are always respected.

3. Monitoring and Feedback

A major weakness in our globalisation strategies is improper monitoring and inadequate feedback. Our diplomatic missions through the commercial attaches should take greater interest in our foreign business presence. They should constantly give feedback to the government of India on the progress of business ventures so that appropriate policy redirections can be attempted. "Country Risk Analysis" should be an integral part of the international business divisions of companies global checklist of the performance of enterprises in various regions of the world should be made, so that lessons can be learnt from both successes and failures coordinated country-specific policy evaluation of both private and public sector overseas ventures should be made, so that lessons can be learnt from both successes and failures. A coordinated country-specific policy evaluation of both private and public sector overseas ventures should be undertaken by the Commerce Ministry in style of the celebrated Japanese MITI (Ministry of International Trade and Industry). This synergetic networking of expertise can be immensely useful in strengthening our globalisation efforts.

India also has several overseas joint ventures, which promote not only trade but also investment-based economic cooperation. These joint ventures are in diverse fields and in many countries particularly in West Asia and SouthEast Asia.Along with these joint ventures, collaborations in the form of consultancies, transfer of know-how and management skills have acquired new dimensions. Indian ventures have made efforts to adapt first world technology to the needs of the third world and to impart management know-how in diverse fields including power generation, construction of civil projects, railway operation and other technical services. Such consultancies have been successful in Africa and West Asia.They need to be expanded.

Globalization and Reforms an Indian Perspective

Globalization involves both interdependence and integration with the rest of the world.

Globalization is an attempt by India to join the industrialized and free market economies of the world. It involves discarding the traditional approaches to managing the economy and a massive social and economic experiment with little parallels in history.

The "Strategic Intent" of India must be to become one of the Sixth largest economies of the world. Accomplishing the "strategic intent" of joining a select group of leading economies calls for effective leadership, political will and a shared national agenda.

It must be remembered that India has several advantages—

1. A stable and vibrant democracy
2. Wide use of the English Eanguage
3. Avalability of world-class scientific, technical, managerial and professional manpower.

4. Established Western style corporate democracy and a functioning legal system for grievance redress and contract enforcement
5. A growing and sizable middle-class estimated at 200 million.

India should effectively capitalize on these advantages in its quest to globalize.

India's experiment with hybrid markets - not centrally planned or subject to market mechanisms may create structural impediments to change. India can rapidly build on its private sector capabilities, and public sector physical infrastructure. However, transition to a market economy will demand that proceses that distorted market forces during the last thirty-five years —"the licence-quota Raj" be eliminated.

The recent developments against globalization in Geneva, Seattle, Washington, Prague or Davos have proved that there is an alliance between ultra leftist as well as ultra rightist militants with narrow nationalist outlloks. Indian farmers were joined by Swiss farmers having opposite interests at the WTO meetings in Geneva in 1999.It should however be kept in mind that the former should benefit from liberalisation of agricultural trade unlike the latter who, with the Japanese are the most protected farmers in the world.

It should also be noted that foreign investors and MNCs are not waiting to rush into India, but they have to be assiduously courted, as there is worldwide competition for foreign capital. MNCs no longer represent the demonic face of capitalism today.

Massive public funds are needed for much better operations and maintenance expenditure in the power and transport sectors.

The miserable conditions of power supply in Kerala or New Delhi or deteriorating network of roads all over India require massive public investments, which cannot be got by domestic investment alone.

Globalization is not solely responsible for the poverty still prevailing in the LDCs. In India, one hears complaints of the lack of a 'human face' to economic reforms. In "Green Revolution'

Villages, poverty is retreating and reforms favour the overall movement of the economy. In sluggish areas, reforms are hardly felt and conditions of the poor hardly change. The 'Roots' of poverty have little to do with globalization and reforms. Questions have to be asked to local politicans about the failure of 'reforms' in their States.The plains of Bihar could again be the granaries of India as they were with Bengal for a few thousand years till the end of the nineteenth century if proper policies are enforced.

In the past ten years, India has been removing barriers to trade, FDI and foreign financial investment. The open market-guided economy has been far more efficient than the command economy. The economy has being growing at a steady growth rate of over 6%, experiencing only moderate inflation and taken all kinds of shocks - the East Asian and Russian crashes and rising oil prices in its stride.

Tables 1, 2 & 3 show India's attempts at Globalization.There have been a perceptible increase in FDI, Foreign Collaborations and NRI Investments.

It should be kept in mind that while the "Nehruvian Strategy"had historical significance giving the Indian economy a certain depth and spread, and lent the Indian economy and society the dignity it did not possess after the colonial experience it had negative features, which required a change in strategy. Over time connections were rewarded rather than enterpreneuial flair. Crony capitalism rather than socialism distorted the production structure.

Today there is abroad consensus across the political spectrum that reforms should continue, although there are differences in the pace and sectoral calibration.

Globalization has to be to our advantage and we should be clever enough to exploit the needs of the industrialized world and play one mega unit against the other.

When an integrated pattern of relationship between different sectors in industry and trade emerges our economy will itself become Global in the true sense.

Foreign investment no longer represents the demonic face of capitalism.

While concepts of sovereignty are changing in an increasingly interdependent globalised world, foreign companies are more than careful in conforming to legal codes and national laws in their host countries.

The Chinese who not long ago, accused foreigners of being the running dogs of imperialism, who should be wiped out from the face of the earth, are now welcoming foreign investment with open arms.

Today there is a realisation that in a competitive environment, effort, enterprise and innovation can bring about economic transformation.

Criticisms about the new directions in economic policy have come both from left-leaning academicians and ultra-right wing parties. It is indded ironic that while the Marxists in Government have realized the importance of the market mechanism to allocate resources, some left-wing academicians and leading intellectuals in our left-of—centre universities have raised unwarranted criticisms against economic reforms. These" drawing room Cassandra's" and "arm-chair Marxists", who are now bereft of any ideological moorings, with the demise of Communism, and who are denied lucrative foreign assignments or Government sinecures, like in the planning commission, have taken up Government-baiting as their principal occupation.

It must also be remembered that everything is not hunky-dory with economic reforms or the direction in which our polity is heading under the current dispensation. While at the macro-economic policy level the reforms are progressing in a reasonably satisfactory manner, it is at the micro -implementation level of translating policy into reality, that there are serious lacunae, which can derail the entire globalization-reform process. Senior-level bureaucrats are not ready to give up their discretionary powers to arbitrate between producers and consumers, while lower-level functionaries continue to play an obstructionist role. Inter-ministerial co-ordination needs to be fine-tuned much more. Our grass-root institutions need drastic over-hauling to see that the benefits of reforms and globalization percolate down to the poorer sections, and should be more accountable and responsive to their needs.

Politicians in power (besides a few committed Ministers and Chief-Ministers) continue to behave in a feudal manner. Corruption, Nepotism and vasf'patronage networks" still exist. The colonial mind-set still pervades many of our Leaders and bureaucrats, who believe in a patron-client relationship of granting favours to stay in power and wielding influence, rather than service to the people as their representatives. There is need for serious introspection by our policy-makers, if India wants to be in the front ranks in the comity of nations.

New Trends in the Indian Economy

The "Economic Survey" for 2003-2004 has described the need to devise strategies to raise industrial growth to over 10% as one of the most important challenges of the country's economic policy.

Highlighting the fact that industry has grown only by single digit ever since 1995-96,it says there *are five* ***major constraints*** in the way of raising industrial output to the required levels. These are-

1. Small scale sector reservation,
2. High customs tariffs,
3. Rigidities in labour laws,
4. Frictions in creation and closure of firms
5. Distortions in the structure of indirect taxes.

India has experienced a steadily deepening globalisation and Indian firms are- getting integrated into global production chains. India's best firms are today globally competitive and realising rapid export growth rates. As for foreign direct investment (FDI), there has been slow down over the last few years. FDI is important not only for the funds brought in, but also for the technological know how, improved corporate governance practices and access to foreign markets.

As for cuts in customs tariff, India should move towards gradually reducing duty rates and aligning them with that of ASEAN countries.

FDI inflows in the country peaked at $4.74 billion in 2000-01,declined thereafter to $3.73 billion in 2002-03 and further to $3.57 billion in 2003-04.This is against $52.7 billion recorded by China in 2002.Decline in FDI was principally on account of a sharp drop in net equity flows. Export promotion policies need to utilize the natural complementarity of FDI with export activity. The global reach and marketability of FDI could be effectively utilized to provide a cutting edge to export effort.

India has gone through more than a decade of economic reforms. Beginning in 1991,the thrust of reforms was fiscal stabalisation, and initiation of major structural reforms aimed at industrial de-regulation and globalisation to induce accelerated ***investment, growth*** and employment. The financial sector reforms have been brought into balance with sustainable balance of payments, foreign currency assets at $150 billion, and a comfortable servicing of debt-repayments. Inflation levels are at record lows of less than 5% in the last five years, and poverty has fallen from 36% in the early 1990s to less than 26% in 2001-2002.However, there have been major infrastructural bottlenecks-inadequate good-quality roads and lack of serious reforms in the power sector. The Information Technology (IT) sector has also made rapid strides, and India has emerged as a key player in IT and IT-enabled services.

The key disappointment of the 1990s has been inadequate employment generation-with employment elasticities rapidly coming down in the organised sector. There has also been an "absolute" fall in agricultural employment.

Second generation Reforms have already been initiated, and it is hoped that acceleration in economic growth and exports will follow, without significant changes in the socio-political parameters. India is now focusing on labour-market reforms and disinvestment in the public sector, besides speeding up the liberalisation and globalisation process.

Conclusions

India can strive to become a global player if it keeps in mind the following factors—

1. Develop a pro-active mind-set and agenda for effective globalization.
2. Target specific industries for special concessions
3. Focus on quality as a national priority.
4. Allow Indian firms to invest in building marketing and service infrastructure in select markets.
5. Recognise bad loans and clean up the banking system.
6. Pay attention to the political processes in the industrialised countries.
7. Build up a strong anti-dumping secretariat outside the government to collect data on international costs and profitability in the production of consumer goods that will soon be freed from QRs (Quantitative Restrictions)
8. Reform of the Labour market and a proper exit policy for loss-making enterprises.

In the final analysis, a strong and vibrant democracy with women, rural poor and the oppressed classes waking up to the realization of the assertion of political power, can take a globalised India to greater economic heights.

9

BUILDING BRIDGES ACROSS BORDERS—THE ISLAMABAD SUMMIT AND THE SAARC PROCESS

As a consequence of the Islamabad SAARC Summit of 2004, and the Indo-Pakistan dialogue, Pakistan seems to be at long last looking for a realistic solution to the Kashmir dispute. There is thus a "Paradigm shift" in that country's "bleed India" policy. However, experience of the past shows that any forward movement in peace initiatives is followed by retracting to old positions of animosity and hostility. Pakistan often talks peace, while preparing for war. It is hoped that the "war of attrition" in Kashmir will be given a final burial. The raison-de-atre of the Pakistan State should change from being a "spoiler" of India's progress. Pakistan should not insist on Kashmir as the core issue and progress with talks with India sequentially, but veer around to the Indian viewpoint that talks should progress simultaneously on all issues, including economic co-operation. Economic co-operation can bind the two nations together, unlike politics, which will create further divisions and mutual distrust.

Whatever be the motives, Pakistan is moving at a pace no one had dreamt of before. The voices within Pakistan urging the establishment to look for a way out of the Kashmir imbroglio are feeble, but growing. This could mean that the high-pitched decades-old rhetoric is toned down. Negotiations, from a Pakistan point of view should be conducted with India on a LOC (Line of Control) plus solution that allows for some territorial adjustments and soft borders, and possibly a ten-mile deep de-militarized zone. While the division of Kashmir is unfortunate, it is better to accept this reality, than live with endless suffering that has consumed almost a million lives since the 1980s.

However, there is a growing feeling in Pakistan that the country is being made to give in too much, without anything in return from India. It is hoped that once the "composite dialogue" gets underway, the feeling that India is extracting concessions from Pakistan without commensurate benefits is put to rest.

Another important question is will President Pervez Musharraf face the same fate as Anwar Sadat of Egypt from the jihadis. His jihad against the jihadis may prove counterproductive.

India infact has never shared the West's confidence in Musharraf or the belief that Pakistan after Musharraf would be ruled only by nuke-wielding jihadis.

In its assessment, the Indian government feels there is unlikely to be any change in Pakistan's position vis-a –vis India. Kashmir is not about to be toppled off its pedestal, and a significant component of the Pakistan military-intelligence establishment will continue to subscribe to the bleed India theory.

Given the poor state of the Pakistan economy, anyone who comes to power in Pakistan is likely to be more vulnerable to the same pressures from the U.S and other Western powers.

The 12th Summit of SAARC took place in the context of complex social, economic and political developments globally and regionally. The slowing down of global trade negotiations under W.T.O, a "shining India", and in some measure South Asia, the success of formations like ASEAN, the increasing international pressure to combat terrorism and resolve regional conflicts and regional security concerns have contributed to making regionalism not an option, but a necessity especially among LDCs with a burgeoning growth potential. But in the past, SAARC nations have been lackadaisical about implementing the high-sounding commitments of Summit declarations. The question to be asked is –"Is there any reason to believe that the Islamabad summit has discovered the magic that will hasten the pace towards regional integration"?

As has often been pointed out, SAARC is after all a unique regional group in many ways and especially because one country, India constitutes a centrality that is physical, geographical and economic. And there lies the core of the problem. The strongest gains of regionalism naturally accrue to India. It is for India to ensure that smaller members of the region have a growing stake in regionalism as well. This responsibility India has taken seriously. For example SAFTA (South Asia Free Trade Agreement) envisages the liberalisation of commodity trade as a key issue, with trade in services following. As critics have pointed out, this would have little appeal to smaller nations, which only feel threatened by the flooding of goods from India, with the removal of barriers. Little effort has been made to ensure necessary protection to the least developed countries of the region. It is here that enlarging co-operation in areas such as education and health services can create synergies. It is also a cause for concern that SAARC agreements on co-operation on other issues, which attract no barriers, have not taken off. In 1992, the "Poverty Commission Report of SAARC" set targets for the eradication of poverty in South Asia.All that has happened is that is that in 2002,another commission was constituted, that has come up with further recommendations. Nor have SAARC nations registered a commendable record in other areas of possible co-operation. Under the "Integrated Programme of Action", there has not been a single co-operative project to harness hydro potential in the region to mutual benefit despite talk of sub-regional co-operation through growth triangles or quadrangles between India's northeast, Bangladesh, Bhutan and Nepal.

Now coming to the prospects of a South Asian Union and the stages of integration in the SAARC region.

The region actually has an edge because of its common history. Before 1947, we had a single currency and an integrated market.

As regards the road map to economic integration-

1. Free Trade Area

Agreement has been signed to set-up a SAFTA by 2006.This will involve abolition of quantitative restrictions and reduction of import tariffs to about 5% on each other's products.

2. Customs Union

In a free trade area, there are chances of possible leaks in the system. That is a country could import a product, then re-export it to another country, where tariffs are higher-customs union will take care of all situations. In a customs union there is a common external tariff.

3. Common Market

All restrictions on cross-border movements of labour, technology transfer are removed. There is a sharing of capital, resources and management. Common patrolling of borders and investing agencies working in tandem. There will be open-borders with travel without visas.

4. Economic Union

In economic union there is a common currency, harmonisation of fiscal and monetary policy.

5. Political Union

Harmonise security and foreign policy Common South Asian parliament is also mooted.

Regarding the pros and cons of South Asian integration—On the positive side, Indo-Pak trade may touch $ 10 billion within 5 years of SAFTA.Integrated economies and markets will make South Asia an attractive destination for FDI.It will promote the sub-continent's civilisational harmony and cultural contiguity. Free from the burden of regional dissonance, India will be better equipped to play a larger legitimate role in world affairs.

On the flip side, the disadvantages would be India would have to constantly bend backwards to accommodate other smaller neighbours. Also, India's natural strategic compass is broader than South Asia, and extends from the Straits of Hormuz to the Malaccan Straits, with a pre-eminent role as a global power. Open borders also may spell trouble-we will have a flood of illegal immigrants particularly from Bangladesh and Pakistan, which may retard the Indian economy.

Coming to the specifics of SAFTA, it is on the whole a welcome step, as tariff barriers in the region are all artificial. However, the duration of the process is too long. The process starts in 2006.and continues for another 6 to 8 years before the tariffs are actually brought down to the minimum range. The pace is much slower than the W.T.O route, and not keeping in pace with worldwide liberalisation trends. Sri Lanka has a FTA (Free Trade Agreement) with India and Pakistan, and will be initialling one with Bangladesh shortly.

In the current global context of regionalism, SAFTA will attract wider global attention in view of the combined huge market size and the growth potential of the region in terms of available resources.

South Asia has multiple heterogeneities-namely geographical, economic, political and social. The region doesn't lack resources, but lacks initiatives for building complementarities.

SAARC region continues to remain a hub of poverty, large unemployment, and economic backwardness. On the macro-economic front, all the major economies suffer from large fiscal deficits; expenditure increases on account of defence and security.

SAARC was established in 1986 as recognition of the imperative for a wider and broad-based regional co-operation forum encompassing cultural, social, economic and technical fields. However, SAARC couldn't make much headway ever since its inception, as each country followed a development strategy independent of others, without any policy co-ordination. Intra-SAARC trade has made little headway so far. In 2003,intra-SAARC trade (exports+imports) was around 5% of the total trade of the region. India accounts for 71% of intra-SAARC exports (mainly to Bangladesh, Nepal and Sri Lanka). Bangladesh accounts for 36% of intra-SAARC imports, due to large imports from India.

Even if India is a dominant economy in SAARC it makes tremendous economic sense to enter into co-operation with India.Since India is an emerging fast moving economy, the smaller countries can stand to benefit immensely by accessing the large domestic market of India. It should give them great opportunities for developing their economies, particularly agriculture and industry.

However, we should also integrate investment with trade. Bangladesh will sell to India in a free trade environment Dacca saris or hilsa fish, in which it has a competitive advantage and ready demand in India. But; this will be a lop-sided trade practice, defeating the very process. If India invests in gas-based projects in Bangladesh, and later imports gas from that country, it will be much more meaningful in a South Asian context.

Apart from trade, there will be the larger "peace and stability dividend". There will be region-wide growth, peace and harmony and a more conducive environment for investment, employment, effective resource mobilisation and utilisation for all countries.

A breakthrough in Indo-Pak bilateral relations is more good news for the "economic health" of the region, and will vindicate intra-SAARC trade liberalisation. Pharmaceuticals, engineering goods, power and infrastructure are areas of immediate intra-regional co-operation.

Will SAFTA work in the long run? Today, NAFTA is working well, EUs (European Union) single market and single currency have been very successful and of course ASEAN is working very well. There is thus reason to hope that SAARC will also be successful.

As regards SAPTA (South Asian Preferential Tariff Area) introduced in 1995, so far a total of 5,550 tariff lines have been earmarked for concessional tariffs by all countries, and value addition norm has been reduced from 50% to 40%. SAFTA has been perceived as a transition from SAPTA, through gradual progress in tariff concessions.

The progress in SAPTA was stymied and marred by apprehension, especially in Bangladesh and Pakistan, regarding possible flooding of goods from India.The focus of the trade dialogue within the region is dominated more by the desire to balance bilateral trade, than by the desire to promote trade. This comes in the way of growth of trade and affects progress on SAPTA/SAFTA.

Intra-SAARC investments are not very significant. Instead of co-operating among themselves, they have been competing to attract FDI.There is lack of dynamism at present in the intra-SAARC trade relationship.

It is hoped with the thawing of Indo-Pak relations, and the operationalisation of SAFTA, a big boost to trade and investment flows within SAARC will begin.

In conclusion, if hostilities can create nuclear powers in the region, co-operation will create economic powers.

Table 1

Significance of SAARC to member countries

SAARC country	*Total exports (In US $ (billion)*	*Exports to SAARC (%)*	*Total Imports (In US billion)*	*Imports from SAARC (%)*
Bangladesh	4.69	1.9%	8.36	12.7%
India	42.10	4.8%	51.63	0.9%
Nepal	0.80	2.7%	1.37	34.3%
Pakistan	9.03	3.2%	11.29	2.7%
Sri Lanka	5.43	3.5%	6.32	11.2%

Table 2

Economics of South Asia, 2002

SAARC COUNTRY	*Population (in million)*	*GNP (US $ billion)*
Bangladesh	136	48.5
Bhutan	0.851	0.5
India	1048	501.5
Maldives	0.28	0.59
Nepal	24	5.6
Pakistan	145	59.2
Sri Lanka	19	15.9

Table 3

Growth Rates of Intra-SAARC Trade (%)

SAARC country	*Total exports*	*Exports to SAARC*	*Total Imports*	*Imports from SAARC*
Bangladesh	9.9	6.5	10.5	10.1
India	9.1	12.0	11.5	19.8
Nepal	14.2	53.5	5.3	29.7
Pakistan	3.4	2.9	4	12.4
Sri Lanka	9.2	14.1	4.8	6.2
SAARC 5	8.2	11.7	9.4	12.4

Source: for all Tables-WORLD DEVELOPMENT REPORT, 2004.

10

REGIONAL COOPERATION IN THE INDIAN OCEAN RIM

The IOR-ARC (Indian Ocean Rim Association for Regional Cooperation), the latest grouping, of which India is a member, came into existence in March 1997 after initial meetigs, called the "Mauritius Initiative". It consists of fourteen countries- Australia, India, Indonesia, Kenya, Madagascar, Malaysia, Mauritius, Mozambique, Oman, Singapore, South Africa, Sri Lanka, Tanzania and Yemen.At the second meeting of the Council of Ministers of the IOR-ARC in Maputo, Mozambique in March 1999, it was decided to admit five more members: Bangladesh, Iran, Seychelles, Thailand and the United Arab Emirates. The Council of Ministers is the Apex Body of IOR-ARC; besides there are two other bodies – IORBF- [Indian Ocean Rim Business Forum] and IORAG [Indian Ocean Rim Academic Group] (These come under what is called the non-governmental Track-2 initiatives).

The initial euphoria of forging Indian Ocean Rim cooperation is today on the wane. It is claimed that IOR-ARC has enormous economic potential and offers considerable trade and investment opportunities. South Africa is rich in minerals and is a major economic power in Africa. East Africa has enormous tourist potential. South Asia has abundant skilled manpower and untapped markets. South East Asia is an Economic Powerhouse, and Australia is rich in natural resources and a developed country. However, it must be remembered that the Indian Ocean Region comprises a collection of economically diverse and disparate countries. It is characterized by significant variations in levels of wealth and economic development, economic and trade interests, including dependence on regional trade, and political interest in regional cooperation. Australia, Singapore and United Arab Emirates fall in the high-income category. Malaysia, Mauritius, Oman, Seychelles and South Africa are in the upper middle-income category. Indonesia, Iran, Sri Lanka and Thailand fall in the lower middle-income category. Finally, Bangladesh, India, Kenya, Madagascar, Mozambique, Tanzania and Yemen belong to the low-income category. These low-income countries, with the exception of India and Kenya are among the least developed countries of the world. A country like Mozambique with one of the lowest per-capita incomes in the world has little in common with a high growth country like Singapore.

IOR-ARC member countries actively participate in the global trading environment at the commercial and political level. Exports from IOR-ARC countries to all markets grew almost 500% in the 90s, almost six times their previous level, but Singapore-Malaysia trade dominates IOR-ARC trade. IOR-ARC controls only 10.7% of the world trade, and intra-regional trade amounts to 18.5%, and thus it is not in a position to dominate global trade liberalization. There is little potential for member countries of the Indian Ocean region to deepen economic linkages and increase trade and investment flows. Studies show that trade increases were not linked to the formation of the IOR-ARC.

Approaches to regional cooperation will therefore be heavily influenced by these considerations.

The history of regional cooperation suggests that regional arrangements involve a dynamic process, often developing from relatively modest proposals, when compared with their subsequent evolution. This has been the case with the European Union (EU), and more recently the North American Free Trade Area (NAFTA).

Regional Arrangements vary in their scope and depth of integration. At one extreme, they may be no more than informal consultative forums. More advanced, yet still shallow, forms of integration involve preferential trading arrangements, which extend lower tariff preferences to members than to non-members.

Preferential arrangements may also include agreements on investments, standards and other regulatory issues.

Deeper forms of integration involve the formation of a single economics area behind common external tariffs. Such arrangements may extend to national governments ceding trade policy to a supra-national body, and pursuing the harmonisation of their micro and macro policies. The European Union (EU) is such a type of regional organization.

Regional arrangements may be driven either by market or political imperatives, or more usually some combination of both. All regional arrangements and other forms of regional cooperation can be positioned along a continuum from market- driven, to politically driven integration. At the far market-driven end, would be integration in the South China Region (Guangdong, Fujian, Taiwan and Hong-Kong), where the economies of Taiwan and the Mainland, do not recognise each other politically. At the far end of the policy-driven arrangements, with little market basis to integration, are many of the formal economic arrangements in Latin America and Africa in the 1960s and 1970s.

The IOR-ARC is based on the concept of Open Regionalism, which is distinct from Preferential Regionalism .In Preferential Regionalism trade preferences are given to members at reduced tariffs. This results in a net positive impact on trade among members. It may also have a negative impact or no effect on trade with non-members due to trade diversion. Regional co-operation, which promotes the benefits of closer regional ties, but without any discriminatory trade measures, is Open regionalism. Simply put, open regionalism is trade liberalisation among the member countries in the region on a most favoured nation (MFN) basis unilaterally without asking for reciprocity from non-members.

It is argued that open regionalism is a flexible arrangement that is more member friendly than neo-liberalist regional arrangements such as preferential trading arrangements, free trade areas etc. There are no laws and binding contracts and decisions are made by consensus. Compliance to any commitment is voluntary and there is no rigid institutional structure and bureaucratic set-up to specify obligations.

Integration of the IOR will depend on the complementarity –in terms of resources, skills, markets, investment flows of the countries of the region, and policy reforms (particularly domestic economic reform policies), that provide trade and investment opportunities. There are no binding contracts, and decisions are made by consensus. There is considerable confusion about the implications and relevance of Open –regionalism. The logic of the case of economic benefits to be won by unilateral liberalization is weak. There is always reluctance to comprehensive reduction of trade barriers. With unstructured arrangements, coordination is limited. A dialogue-oriented forum will not be as successful in economic terms as an action-oriented regional bloc will. Project-driven confidence-building measures will not be sufficient to sustain a regional grouping.

The basic ingredients for effective market integration to support open-regionalism are not in place in the IOR-ARC. Only that part of the IOR-ARC that strongly benefited from FDI was South East Asia sub-region and to a lesser extent Australia.The analysis of trade flow statistics show that the expected spin-off of accelerated economic growth in these regions have not permeated the larger region.

In the current IOR-ARC agenda, there are projects under various working groups. Some of them have made considerable progress and reached a stage of recommending various sector –related policy proposals. These projects can be categorised into two broad areas: (*a*) trade and investment facilitation and (*b*) economic and technical co-operation. The projects are on: standards and accreditation, investment facilitation and promotion trade promotion, improvement in maritime transport, human resource development, tourism promotion and development. The follow up on projects has been very tardy.

IOR covers too many individual countries, with significant differences in factor endowments. Similar economic structures mean limited trade opportunities. There are also limited complementarities in terms of savings-most of the economies are borrowers- and in terms of supply and demand for advanced capital goods and technology.

Almost 90% of intra-IOR-ARC trade and its growth come from the Southeast Asian countries. North and East African and Indian Ocean Island sub-groups have contributed only marginally to intra-IOR-ARC trade and its growth. The analysis of trade flow statistics shows that the expected spin-off of accelerated economic growth in these regions has not permeated the larger region.

The Indian Ocean group is much too disparate and scattered to make a mark in the near future. South Africa has its own African commitments, has a sagging interest in IOR-ARC and is overburdened by regional pulls in its immediate neighbourhood. There are renewed financial problems in South East Asia, and the economies have once again slowed down, after recovering from the financial crisis of 1997.Australia has a reluctant "look west" policy, and continues her close ties with the Pacific-particularly the United States. Moreover, Australia was interested in the IOR-ARC, more from a security/defence perspective rather than economic cooperation. Mauritius and Oman are active in the IOR-ARC, because they need more economic space to assert themselves. Mauritius is better known for routing questionable foreign investment through its shores to India-known as the "Mauritius Route". In any case such grandiose schemes of regional cooperation spanning three Continents-from Canberra to Cape Town, with Calcutta along the way are far too ambitious too be economically viable.

The influence of the Indian diaspora in promoting intra-IOR trade and directing it to India has also been minimal, unlike the Chinese and their strong GUANXI (networking contracts) with a lasting contribution to the development of Mainland China.Compliance to any commitment is voluntary and there is no rigid institutional structure to enforce obligations.

As regards the so-called Track2 initiatives, the IORAG also has not contributed much to furthering Rim cooperation. The Chair in

Indian Ocean Studies at Mauritius is lying vacant for sometime now. External Affairs Ministry officials say that the academic inputs to policymaking were inadequate, but the fact is that South Block mandarins are also not too enthusiastic about the IOR-ARC

Bilateral initiatives will yield greater flows of trade, than over-ambitious regional cooperation plans. To increase India's share of merchandise exports from the stagnant 0.7% to a higher level, sustained export promotion should be the constant endeavour of the government. These should include reduction in transaction costs through decentralisation, simplification of procedures, and identification of thrust sectors. Measures such as special economic zones, promotion of agricultural exports, market access initiatives, setting up business cum trade facilitation centres/trade portals and duty free replenishments, should be pursued with renewed vigour. India should further intensify her trade with the European Union and select ASEAN countries like Malaysia and Singapore, where there are new opportunities emerging in the post-WTO accord world. Bilateral Free Trade Pacts like India has with Nepal and Sri Lanka should be encouraged.

Thus India should focus her economic diplomacy on deepening bilateral engagement and FTAs (Free Trade Agreements) rather than in pursuing regional cooperation with an amorphous and heterogeneous group of countries, like in the Indian Ocean region.

11

INDO-AUSTRALIAN COMMERCIAL TIES

Background

Destination India seems to be the latest buzzword in business circles Down Under.Though India is placed at "unlucky" 13th position of the total international trade of Australia at present.the Australian Trade Commission feels that the country can well share the first position in a few year's time.

Traditionally, Australian companies have focused on Far-eastern nations like China, Indonesia, Japan, Singapore, Thailand and Korea due to logistical advantage and lower tariffs. But now, the Australian giants have realised India's huge market potential.

As an indicator, Australia's trade with China stands at nearly four times that of India.However, India is now being perceived as the "second" China due to its huge market size. Going by the present trends, it is expected that India will equal China in about five year's time.

The sectors that have attracted attention are minerals, specialised telecom and IT hardware, and processed foods, fruits and vegetables. However, emerging areas include environment management products, medical hardware, health consultancy services, hospital management, tourism, film production and specialized IT software.

Infrastructure sector is another area that is seeing participation of Australian companies. Three Australian companies are participating in Sahara Group's flagship project, Amby Valley, in terms of designing and development.

Similarly, several Indian companies are also vying for the Australian market. Birla and Sterlite have recently bought two mines in Australia.Other sectors attracting Indian corporates include IT, minerals, and steel and steel products. Nearly A$ 0.87 billion is currently flowing from India to Australia.

The Australian and Indian Governments are dedicated to improving competitiveness and to building greater links between their Economies and regional and global economies. They are also giving a more active role to business. Regulatory burdens that Government has in the past placed upon business are being drastically reduced. These reforms will further strengthen their economies and their bilateral commercial ties.

The private sector has responded strongly to the new environment. These reform processes have put Australia and India in a position where they are very competitive in Asia-Pacific markets. India has recognised that economic dynamism can only be achieved by releasing the energies of the private sector, and by integrating with the world economy. India's influence in East Asia and the broader Asia-Pacific region will only grow in the years ahead. The pattern of trade too has shifted, with India's exports to the Asia-Pacific region far outpacing the growth of exports to any other region.

Indo-Australian Bilateral Engagement—An Overview

In the *post-Pokharan-2* and *post-September 11th* world, Indo-Australian relations have taken on a new meaning. India's "Look east" and "Extended Neighbourhood" policy initiated in the early 1990s, has acquired new dimensions in Australia.Despite past misgivings, India is being recognised "Down Under" as economically, culturally and politically compatible. The shared "British Commonwealth" legacy of parliamentary democratic pluralism, respect for private property and rule-of –the law, and ofcourse the English language, have brought new economic and strategic complementarities to Indo-Australian relations. Australia's "Look West" policy now goes beyond the ASEAN region to include India in her economic and strategic calculations.

There is growing realisation on both sides to step-up economic cooperation. A perception perhaps lingers in Canberra, that India, could become a rival if India is allowed greater access to the Asia-Pacific region; but the emergence of China as a major economic and strategic player in the region, has tempered Australian misconceptions. India's growing diplomatic clout in the ASEAN, her economic dynamism, rapid modernisation and integration with the world economy, will only strengthen Indo-Australian relations.

Thus, from a phase of "benign neglect", the two countries have reached the stage of "realisation of the potential". India is now certainly more than a small "blimp" on Australia's economic and strategic radar screen.

The Australian and Indian Economies-An Update

The Indian Economy-Reforming and Globalising.

India has gone through more than a decade of economic reforms. Beginning in 1991,the thrust of reforms was fiscal stabalisation, and initiation of major structural reforms aimed at industrial de-regulation and globalisation to induce accelerated investment, growth and employment.

The financial sector reforms have been brought into balance with sustainable balance of payments, foreign currency assets at $100 billion, and a comfortable servicing of debt-repayments. Inflation levels are at record lows of less than 5% in the last five years, and poverty has fallen from 36% in the early 1990s to less than 26% in 2001-2002.However, there have been major infrastructural bottlenecks-inadequate good-quality roads and lack of serious reforms in the power sector. The Information Technology (IT) sector has also made rapid strides, and India has emerged as a key player in IT and IT-enabled services.

The key disappointment of the 1990s has been inadequate employment generation-with employment elasticities rapidly coming down in the organised sector. There has also been an "absolute" fall in agricultural employment.

Second generation Reforms have already been initiated, and it is hoped that acceleration in economic growth and exports will follow, without significant changes in the socio-political parameters.

India is now focussing on labour-market reforms and disinvestment in the public-sector, besides speeding up the liberalisation and globalisation process.

The Australian Economy-Liberalising Frontiers

Australia's open free-market economy was further liberalised in 1988,with the federal Governments' financial de-regulation of the economy. Trade rationalisation in consonance with APEC (Asia-Pacific Economic Co-operation) guidelines, competition policies, labour market reforms, and accelerating overall competitiveness, are some of the other features of the Australian economy in the new millennium.

The Australian economy has shifted away from dependence on resources (particularly mining) and agriculture-based industries to a wide range of financial and service-oriented industries. The biggest growth areas are IT-development, where Australia, like India is in some areas, well into the forefront of the new-technology age.

Australia's open and efficient regulatory environment, sound legal system for dispute-settlement and contract-enforcement has placed it well to attract foreign investment. She has an increasingly large pool of professionals working in IT, engineering, legal, accounting, and management consulting, gelling well with the old economy sectors of mining, oil and gas and agri-business.

Australia is no longer reliant upon exports of agricultural and mining products. It is now increasingly a source of high-value added manufactures and services. Trade now amounts to fully 40% of Australia's GDP-up from 30% only ten years ago. Manufactures now total over 30% of merchandise exports. Services amount to nearly a quarter of all exports. These Reform processes have put Australia in a position, where it is now very competitive in Asia-Pacific markets.

Bilateral Trade

The commodity composition and geographic destination of Indian Exports and Imports is shown in Table-1.

Table 1

Direction of Indian Exports (%share in total)

Region	*% Share in Total*
European Union	26%
Australia	1.2%
United States	21.8%
Japan	4.9%
Russia	2.1%
Africa	3.5%
Asia (ASEAN+China+SAARC)	19%
Latin America and Caribbean	2%

Source—Government of India Economic Survey, 1999-2000

Table 2

Direction of India's Imports (% share in total)

Region	*% Share in Total*
European Union	25.6%
United States	8.7%
Australia	3.6%
Japan	5.7%
Africa	3.8%
Asia (ASEAN+China+South Korea)	15.7%

Source—Government of India "economic survey", 1999-2000

From these two TABLES, it is evident that Australia has a 1.2-% share in India's Exports, and a 3.6% share in India's Imports.

Principal Indian **Exports** to Australia are—

- Textiles and Clothing
- Chemicals and related products
- Engineering products
- Leather goods
- Gems and Jewellery
- Processed foods

Principal Indian **Imports** from Australia are—

- Coal, Coking Coal and Mining equipment
- Wool
- Copper
- Base metal and Ores
- Diamonds
- Wheat
- Software
- Automotive components and Services
- Food processing equipment.

Table-3

Bilateral Trade Betweeen India And Australia

(Value in Rs. billion)

	1994-95	1995-96	1996-97	1997-98	1998-99	1999-00	2000-01
Total Bilateral Trade	39.61	46.75	57.17	58.97	77.09	64.25	66.23
India's Exports to Australia	10.88	12.57	13.56	16.28	16.29	17.38	18.48
India's Imports from Australia	28.73	34.18	43.61	55.21	60.79	46.87	47.75
India's Trade Deficit	17.85	21.61	30.05	32.05	44.49	29.49	29.27

Source—PHD Chamber of Commerce and Industry, 2001.

The above Table-3 and Table-4 show the shifting Bilateral Trade between India and Australia, in terms of Exports and Imports and India's Trade Deficit with Australia.

Some observations on Indo-Australian trade are—

1. In the 1990s,Australia's merchandise exports to India grew 50% faster than total export growth of 8%. Primary commodities still dominate Australian exports to India.

Table-4

Composition Of India's Exports To Australia (1994-95 and 2000-01(In $ billion)} & % change for all the years

All Commodities	1994-95	1995-96	1996-97	1997-98	1998-99	1999-00	2000-01	1994-95 346.54	2000-0 405.11
Cotton yarn fabrics, madeups	41.45	8.56	2.52	13.77	-11.73	3.66	0.59	51.03	41.74
RMG of cotton incl. accessories	60.41	-2.48	-5.53	5.76	-15.33	1.70	-2.59	36.08	35.75
Manufactures of metals	38.01	40.13	9.15	-21.06	-17.74	10.48	-9.69	16.09	29.63
Gems and jewellery	57.78	5.82	13.37	54.25	-12.81	48.44	-25.88	18.71	28.74
Machinery & instruments	14.17	1.03	3.15	1.43	12.04	16.41	11.39	12.10	18.73
Drugs, pharma & fine chemicals	-10.35	3.39	48.46	2.55	17.29	80.35	13.56	4.22	15.97
RMG of manmade fibres	19.75	60.02	15.50	84.43	-14.54	2.96	-8.90	4.92	13.43
Marine products	33.54	35.89	-6.91	89.51	84.94	-12.89	66.05	1.94	12.46
Inorg/org/agroChemicals	46.94	27.58	46.47	-34.56	8.77	-16.17	13.22	9.11	11.50
Handicrafts excl handmade carpets	11.91	34.24	44.29	-10.67	3.62	7.30	3.53	5.66	11.27
Leather goods	52.81	17.24	-22.91	17.15	3.98	-20.51	-6.15	13.48	11.07
Electronic goods	49.19	115.53	37.62	15.43	-34.73	167.11	21.31	1.52	11.03
Processed minerals	163.07	-6.90	-4.69	164.62	-38.13	18.74	12.78	5.49	10.68
Transport equipment	83.40	24.85	-6.99	-4.69	164.62	-38.13	18.74	11.66	10.03
Glass/glassware/ceramics	148.06	-50.78	-4.60	7.49	43.02	261.80	16.10	3.10	9.38
Manmade yarn fabrics madeups	20.14	-12.57	4.33	16.05	56.61	11.62	-20.69	5.53	8.12
Carpet handmade	23.13	1.31	9.71	-1.08	-32.39	31.00	-9.07	7.92	7.01
Plastic & linoleum products	9.84	70.65	54.17	4.14	-19.88	-12.72	36.47	2.56	6.70
Natural silk yarn fabric madeups	-27.92	11.50	-5.18	15.74	1.85	49.59	27.46	2.59	6.17
Sports goods								7.38	5.78
Footwear of leather								15.01	5.52
Leather footwear component									5.35
Dyes intermediate								3.59	4.85
Paper/Wood products								2.48	3.70
Cashew								20.12	3.66
Finished leather								7.27	3.35

Source—Foreign Trade and Balance of Payments, Centre for Monitoring Indian Economy, 2001

2. Among primary products, coal continues to be the major export item, with wool, cotton, legumes, copper ores and processed metals also significant.

3. ETMs (Elaborately Transformed Manufactures) mainly mining, machinery, telecommunications equipment and electrical machinery are becoming increasingly significant.

4. By 2000,India was Australia's 12th largest export market, well upon its ranking of between 20th and 25th over the past 20 years.

5. On current growth rates, India will be one of Australia's top ten export markets in the next five years.

Investment-based Cooperation

The FDI (Foreign Direct Investment) Actual Flows versus Approvals in 2000 was 47.7%. The United States and Mauritius-based U.S companies are the principal sources of FDI to India. The share of different sectors in Approved FDI in India is given in Table 5.

Table-5

Share of Different Sectors in Approved Foreign Direct Investment (FDI in Terms of % Share) in India

Power and Fuels	31.2%
Telecommunications	18.2%
Service Sector	6.3%
Transportation	6.1%
Hotels and Tourism	2.0%
Food Processing	4.7%

Source—secretariat For Industrial Approvals, 2001

Thus, the major sectors of FDI in India are in the Infrastructure sector, with food processing, hotels and tourism having a marginal share.

Australian investment in India covers banking and financial services, manufacturing, telecommunications, hotels, mineral processing, food processing, oil and gas and automotive parts. The largest Australian investment in India is the Bank Standard Chartered/ ANZ. Other Australian companies doing business in India are BHP, RTZ-CRA, Telstra and News Corporation and Lumley Technologies.

Indian motor vehicles like the Suzuki Alto and the Maruti Jeep are also making an impression in the Australian markets.

Thus there is vast scope for Indo-Australian bilateral Investment facilitation and co-operation.

Indo-Aussie Business Ties

The Australian domestic market remains small to medium by world standards, and in many of the industries the success and growth factors are from "exports" or "potential exports". Australian tariff barriers have been considerably lowered, and the objective will be to keep on lowering them, so as to make import-substitution competitive and favourable for business development.

Effort has been made by both Governments and Industry Chambers to increase awareness about potential business opportunities. The scenario has changed recently, as India gets access to international money markets for making overseas investment through ADR/GDR issues.

The match between Indian resources and expertise, with those in Australia will often lead to profitable business ventures.

Tourism and the Hospitality industries have been areas that have witnessed considerable growth, and hold lot of future potential.

Sport, Entertainment and their media links are also areas, which can be strengthened in the years to come.

Australia's leading Fosters beer is now bottled in India, and has been proven successful in many cities.

The Indian entertainment industry, particularly Hindi films, has been a major factor in bringing Australia closer to India.The Hindi film "Dil Chata Hai" has made many Indians want to visit Australia, with its projection of Australia's scenic beauty, and particularly the Sydney Opera House.Over twenty Indian movies were shot in

Australia, and many more are in the pipeline. Australia offers some of the most picturesque shooting spots, and post-production facilities for film shooting.

Wrap-up

In conclusion, there is growing realisation by both Australia and India to step-up trade, investments, and dialogue.

However, some of the problem areas are—

- Australian companies face problems on account of obstinate lower-level Indian bureaucrats, who often renege on unwritten commmitments.
- Multifarious clearances are required at various levels stifling any fresh business ideas.
- Australian companies can help India in exploiting its vast mineral resources to India's advantage, as Australia has superior and time-tested expertise in mineral-exploitation.
- Information Technology, Environment Technology, Health and Tourism are some of the areas where Indo-Aussie collaboration can be intensified.
- Australia also offers excellent and reasonable high-quality higher education compatible with the Indian system. Many Indian students now study in Australian Universities, and the educational flow will only grow in the years to come.
- Inter-State differences in environmental norms of India and the fact that Mining is a State subject also hampers greater Australian investment to India.

Thus sustained bilateral economic engagement and strategic interaction can take Indo-Australian relations to a higher diplomatic plane.

References

1. Australian Web-Sites;www.dfat.gov.au and www.ausgovindia.com
2. Barua, Amit; *Renewing Indo-Australian Ties*; Frontline;13th May 2001, pp. 49-50.

3. *Economic Survey*; Government of India, Ministry of Finance, 2000-2001 and 2001-2002.

4. *The Economist*, London, Various Issues, (1999-2000).

5. Jenelle, Bonor, *Australia-India Security Relations: Common Interest or Common Disinterest?* Working Paper, No. 67, New South Wales, Australian Defence Studies Centre, April 2001.

6. Kenneth McPherson, Pai Panandiker and Marika Vicziamy (eds), *Australia and India in the Context of the Indian Ocean and APEC Regions,* Centre for Policy Research, New Delhi, 2000 (Mimeo).

7. *India-New Economy, Old Economy*, Dept. of Foreign Affairs and Trade, Commonwealth of Australia, 2001.

8. Iyer, Nandini, *India and the Indian Ocean,* APH Publishing House, New Delhi, 1985.

9. World Bank, *World Development Reports*, 2000 and 2001.

12

INDIA AND ASEAN : POTENTIAL FOR TOURISM

National boundaries are today shrinking with the inter-linked effects of technology, information flows, foreign capital mobility and above all the movement of people. With all these developments, and the image of India improving in the eyes of the world, the tourism scenario is also witnessing a change for the better. There is steady growth in the value of tourist arrivals, which today stands at about three million foreign tourists. The composition of tourists is also changing, with inflows from Europe, from where the vast majority of tourists come, stagnating, and tourists from Asian countries showing an increasing trend.

Indians are also increasingly traveling abroad in the past-liberalization era, both for work and pleasure. The entry of global brands in India, and international exposure through television has triggered off a desire to travel overseas. The vast increase in 'internet' usage is another factor that has accelerated exposure to the international environment.

Tourism has a lot of potential for expansion both in India and ASEAN countries, and also as an input in Indo-ASEAN services trade. Services, like trade, transport, communication and finance are the traditional components of the tertiary or service sector. Some of the newly emerging services are—

- Financial services
- Marketing and communication services (Media, advertising and consultancy)
- Marketing, logistics, trading and distribution

- Trade promotion services
- Government administration
- Preventive health care services and
- Tourism

Travel and Tourism have emerged as the biggest industry of the millennium, according to John Nesbit in "Global Paradox". Besides direct employment, tourism is a multi-dimensional activity covering a large number of activities, such as travel agencies, souvenir shops, village handicrafts, preservation of historical monuments, and hotels. Tourism is thus a GDP accelerator. The "spread effects" of tourism is thus much wider. Tourism also helps survival of art forms, crafts and culture. Another feature is its contribution to national integration, and enrichment of the social and cultural lives of people. By 2020, there will be 1.6 billion international tourist arrivals worldwide, spending $2000 million on tourism and auxiliary services. Between 2005 and 2010, 250 million new jobs would be created in this sector-200 million of them in the Asia-Pacific region alone.

The tourism revolution which has been sweeping the world since the 1960s has virtually by-passed India. Even after half a century of effort, India's share of the world tourism market has remained at a pathetic 0.45%, while ASEAN countries like Malaysia and Singapore have jumped to visitor counts five to six times our figure.

The common strands in ASEAN countries tourism performance are—

- Political will
- Adequate infrastructure like hotels
- Effective marketing and promotion
- Tourism as a stand-alone activity, rather than an appendage.

China also is forging ahead in tourism promotion and considers tourism as a "pillar of the economy". Tourism in India is placed 51st in the Planning Commission's 52 priorities. However, after some recent pro-active steps by the government of India, tourism has become the third largest foreign-exchange earner after gems and jewelry and ready-made garments, in the form of invisible exports. Tourism's contribution to foreign exchange during 2005 was Rs.175 billion.

It is a well-known fact that tourism and the associated and ancillary services, which it generates, is a bigger money-spinner than the arms and armaments industry. However, only in recent years has the study of tourism and the hospitality industry received wider international attention. Today, hospitality and tourism is a global mega-industry and has been institutionalized as a socio-economic-ecological-cultural phenomenon. Income from tourism has tended to increase at a higher rate than merchandise exports in a number of countries. It acts as an assured channel of finance flow from developed to developing countries with serious balance of payments problems, because of its contributions to the "invisible" item in the Balance of Payments (BOP).

The Principal tourist generating countries in terms of expenditure in dollars worldwide were Germany, U.S., U.K., Japan and France – these top five countries contributed 52.6% of the world total. Table-1 shows the Cross-flows of international tourism in 2004

Table 1 : Flow of International Tourism

Inboud to outbound from	*Africa*	*America*	*Europe*	*West Asia*	*South Asia*
Africa	5.9	0.2	0.8	1.3	-
America	0.6	58.9	18.8	0.7	0.3
Europe	5.6	11.0	240.2	5.8	1.2
West Asia	0.6	0.4	0.7	4.0	0.2
South Asia	-	0.7	0.2	0.6	1.0

Source: Tourism Trends Worldwide: World Tourism Organization, Madrid.

The more liberal vacation policies in big business organizations, greater affluence, and increase in spending among all sections of the people have given rise to an increased emphasis on leisure. The growing need for a change from routine social, business and family pressures has given tourism greater importance. To leverage for the millennium, both the government and private sector need to do the following—

- Improve the quality of service. Tourism being a service industry, the quality of service makes all the difference between competing destinations. A comprehensive HRD programme should cover-

  1. Orientation of staff at airports
  2. Customs facilitation
  3. Guides on a continuous basis.

Hygienic and efficient services will require a high degree of skill management, giving rise to more employment for improving training in diverse segments of the industry. Re-designing the tourism package should include in a greater measure the following

- Adventure tourism-river-rafting, hang gliding
- Wild life tourism
- Culture-specific tourism like - Heritage or Buddhist-circuit tourism –this will be of particular interest to Japan and ASEAN countries like Thailand.
- Create the right "image" abroad, by stressing India's uniqueness as a tourist destination, covering every taste and preference.
- There should be wide publicity and dissemination programme to create awareness of India's diverse tourist attractions by innovative advertisements and promotional brochures.
- The Himalayan Mountains from Leh to Arunachal Pradesh would interest many young tourists from the ASEAN and the West, and should be marketed effectively.
- Due attention should be given to the highly individualistic and dietary selectivity of discerning foreigners, by highlighting India's rich variety of cuisine.
- India's cultural attaches in our embassies abroad should do much more to market India as a "Unique" tourist destination, and should be effective as "cultural ambassadors".
- Easier accessibility by organizing-(1) more charter flights (2) open skies policy-largely implemented with flights to ASEAN

countries increasing (3)cleanliness, timely immigration processing and transparent customer service.

- Branding-will play an increasingly important role when it comes to competition –The East India Hotels, (Oberoi Group), and Indian Hotels (Tatas) should develop proper synergies.
- Attention needs to be given to the small business traveler and IT professionals and their kith and kin, who are increasingly traveling abroad.
- Training facilities for tourist operators, travel agents and others connected with the industry needs to be strengthened to instill greater professionalism.
- The aims of tourism should be –
  1. Physical invigoration
  2. Mental rejuvenation
  3. Cultural enrichment
  4. Spiritual enlightenment

In the ASEAN region, Indonesia, Malaysia, Philippines and Singapore have well developed tourist facilities, with excellent infrastructure. Vietnam is also attracting considerable number of tourists in recent years. A comparison of India and ASEAN economies in world tourism is given in Table-2.

Table 2 : ASEAN and India in World Tourism, 2001.

Country	*World Tourist Arrivals (million)*	*World Tourism Receipts (US $ billion)*
Thailand	10.1	6.7
Singapore	6.7	6.0
Indonesia	5.2	5.4
Malaysia	12.8	4.9
India	2.5	3.0

Source: Tourism Statistics 2001, Ministry of Tourism and Culture, Government of India.

From the above table it is clear that Malaysia attracts the highest number of tourists at 12.8 million, followed by Thailand (10.1 million), Singapore (6.7 million) and Indonesia (5.2 million). India attracted a mere 2.5 million tourists.

In terms of tourism receipts Thailand was the highest earner- US$ 6.7 billion, followed by Singapore-US$ 6 billion,Indonesia-US$5.4 billion and Malaysia-US$5 billion. India's earnings from tourism were a mere US$ 3 billion.

Table 3 : Composition of Indian Visitors to ASEAN in 2001

Country	*Total No. of Visitors (in thousands)*	*Share by Country (%)*
Brunei	6.9	0.9
Cambodia	2.3	0.3
Indonesia	35.0	4.6
Laos	2.7	0.4
Malaysia	143.5	18.8
Myanmar	5.6	0.7
Philippines	15.4	2.0
Singapore	339.8	44.5
Thailand	206.1	27.0
Vietnam	5.8	0.8
Total	763.0	

Source:-www.aseansec.org.

Indian tourists visiting ASEAN has been about 2% of total ASEAN tourist arrivals. Singapore and Malaysia are the most frequented countries in the tourist itinerary of Indians. Indonesia and Thailand are the next most important countries visited by Indian tourists. India ranks ninth among visitor-generating market for ASEAN. Table-3 gives 2001 figures of Indian visitors to ASEAN. The maximum number being to Singapore (44.5%), followed by Malaysia (18.8%).

Visitors from ASEAN to India have increased considerably in recent years, constituting about 3% of total tourist arrivals in India. In 2004, the maximum numbers of visitors to India were from

Malaysia at 45%, followed by Singapore at 32% and Thailand at 15%.A new trend with the liberalization in the economy is the increasing number of business travelers to India from Malaysia and Singapore. India needs to be much more aggressive in attracting tourists from the ASEAN region.

India has vast cultural, cuisine and heritage diversity, but has not explored this to the extent it should in international markets. Singapore and India can exploit their synergies in marketing skills and capital investment for Singapore and promoting India's civilisational diversity.

The cultural attaches of Indian High Commissions in Malaysia and Singapore and the government of India Tourism offices in Singapore and Kuala Lumpur have been co-operating with the local Tourism Promotion boards to promote India-ASEAN tourism. India is being projected not only as a cultural-heritage and holiday destination, but also for health (Ayurveda in Kerala and existence of state of the art reasonably-priced modern health care facilities in Indian cities, particularly Hyderabad) and adventure tourism.

Muslim pilgrims from Malaysia, Singapore and Indonesia are encouraged to halt in India on their way to Saudi Arabia for the Hajj pilgrimage. Indian and ASEAN tourism officials are also encouraging Buddhist tourists particularly from Thailand to visit Indian Buddhist centres in India, particularly in the Indian States of Bihar, Madhya Pradesh and Andhra Pradesh. Malaysia and Singapore are also now co-operating with each other to jointly promote their countries to tourists in India, rather than competing with each other.

Several crucial decisions in the Bali and Vientiane Indo-ASEAN Summits have been taken to permit direct flights by their respective carriers. The Open-Skies policy of India's civil aviation ministry is now being operationalised with private carriers also being allowed to fly to ASEAN countries. Thus greater connectivity between India and ASEAN will go a long way in enhancing two-way tourist inflows, and commercial interaction.

Vietnam, Laos and Cambodia, can also attract an increasing number of tourists, with their heritage sights like Angkor Vat and

Siem-Reap. Brunei and the Philippines can also attract Indian tourists, and India too needs to promote itself in a big way as these two countries are virtually untapped by tourist inflows from both sides.

A business-like pro-active approach is imperative in promoting tourism. An efficient and sound marketing strategy implying a systematic and co-coordinated execution of tourism policy by tourist undertakings-both government and private is needed. A hard sell approach is the need of the hour to jointly market India's and ASEAN's tourism potential and get over the Westerner's view that Asia and India is a land of "snake charmers" and "rope tricks".

Lastly Indian's with higher incomes who travel abroad and interact with foreigners (including in ASEAN countries) tend to run-down India and project a negative image-this does more damage than all other promotional efforts to encourage tourism-this tendency needs to be put to an end, and all those of us who hear such people talking ill of India should severely reprimand them. In conclusion, India and the ASEAN countries have great opportunities to exploit each other's synergies in the tourism sector.

REFERENCES

1. Tourism in India: Trends and Issues—By S.Dharmarajan and Rabindra Seth: Har Anand Publications Pvt. Ltd. New Delhi, 1994.
2. Tourism Promotion and Development: New Advances—by G.S.Batra and R.C.Dangwal, Deep and Deep Publications Pvt. Ltd. New Delhi, 1999.
3. Economic Dimensions of Tourism by R.K.Malhotra, Amol Publications Pvt. Ltd. New Delhi, 1998.
4. Department of Tourism, Government of India, Annual Reports.
5. Tourism Trends World wide, World Tourism Organisation, Madrid.
6. "Economic and Political weekly", Issues 2000-2004.
7. *"The Hindu"* and *"The Business Line"*

13

INDIA AND CHINA—ECONOMIC PARTNERSHIP

India is a vibrant democracy, despite vast religious, caste and economic diversities. China's per capita income began to exceed India's in the 1990s, though forty years earlier, India's was above that of China. India had avoided the pitfalls of the Great Leap Forward and the Cultural Revolution, though after the Reforms of Deng Xiao Ping since 1978, China is way ahead of India in all the economic and social parameters. In 1991, the Indian government initiated economic reforms. India's market-oriented liberalization and removal of industrial licensing and controls resulted in acceleration of GDP to about 6% a year since 1991, among the fastest for any nation, but considerably lower than the Chinese pace of about 9% for the corresponding period.

China's amazing economic success is stunning the world, and China understands how to move with the times like no other country. Its aim is to be a middle-level developed country in the mid-twenty-first century. China is the world's most competitive nation, and its seventh largest exporter. China desires to modernise rapidly by attracting more foreign investment. However, it must be remembered that the share of FDI in total investment in China is less than 8%, reflecting the extent of capital formation in the economy. The entry of China into the WTO will make China a more transparent and less subsidised economy, meaning more market access opportunity in the domestic markets of China. India could be described until recently as a traditional "mixed economy" with a large public sector, but also lot of private entrepreneurship.

China by contrast has been for the most part a command economy, which until recently had a small private sector, and only recognised the legal possibility of home-grown capitalists a few years ago. The Chinese economy has grown at an average annual rate of 9.8% for two-and-half decades, while India's economy has grown at around 5-6% per year over the same period. Chinese growth has been relatively volatile around this trend, reflecting stop-go-cycles of state response to inflation through aggregate credit management. The higher growth in China essentially occurs because of the much higher rate of investment in China. The investment rate in China (investment as a share of GDP) has fluctuated between 35 to 44 percent over the past 25 years, compared to 20% to 26% in India. In fact, the aggregate incremental capital-output ratios (ICORs) have been around the same in both economies. Within this, there is the critical role of infrastructure investment, which has averaged at 19% of GDP in China compared to 2% in India over the 1990s.

China has far more impressive achievements in the social sector than India, as shown in the Table-1 below.

The mantra of China is sharply focused on becoming an economic superpower and hence everything else follows-foreign policy begins and ends with economic policy.

China is creating a national economy, and the result is a massive and painful restructuring of industry and society. Competition across provincial boundaries is becoming a reality. As a result, the country is experiencing deflation, a continual decline in prices. As prices fall, the economy stagnates.

Chinese export growth has been much more rapid, involving aggressive increases on world market shares. This export growth has been based on relocative capital that has been attracted not only by cheap labour but also by excellent and heavily subsidised infrastructure resulting from the high rate of infrastructure investment. In addition, since the Chinese state has also been keen on provision of basic goods in terms of housing, food and cheap transport facilities,

Table 1 : Social Sector Indicators—A Comparison of India and China–2005

Description	*India*	*China*
Gross enrolment ratio in primary schools (%)	99	114
Adult Literacy (%)	65	91
Labour cost per worker in manufacturing($per year)	1,192	729
Education expenditure (%of central govt.expenditure)	13	13 (Excluding dropouts reenrolling)
Physicians(per 1,000 population)	0.4	1
Health expenditure(%of GDP)	5	6
Health expenditure per capita($)	24	49
Contraceptive prevalence rate (%)	52	83
Human Development Index (HDI)	0.602 (HDI Value) 127(Rank)–Year 2003	0.755 (HDI Value) 85(Rank)- Year 2003

Source: TATA Economic Services and Tenth Five Year Plan, Government of India.

this has played an important role in reducing labour costs for employers. In India, the cheap labour has been because of low absolute wages rather than public provision and underwriting of labour costs, and infrastructure development has been minimal. So it is not surprising that it has not really been an attractive location for export –oriented investment, its rate of export growth has been much lower, and exports have not become an engine of growth.

In terms of inequality, in both economies the recent pattern of growth has been inequitable. In China, the spatial inequalities across regions have been the sharpest. In India, vertical inequalities and rural-urban divide have become much more marked. In China recently, as a response to this, there have been some top-down measures to reduce inequality, for example through changes in tax rates, greater public investment in western and interior regions and improved social security benefits. In India, it is political change that has forced greater attention to redressing inequalities, though the process is still very incipient.

In terms of the future prospects, surprisingly, both economies end up with very similar issues despite these major differences. There are clear questions of sustainability of the current pattern of economic expansion in China, based on high export-accumulation model that requires constantly increasing shares of world markets and very high investment rates. Similarly, the hope in some policy quarters in India that information technology-enabled services can become the engine of growth is one, which raises the problems of sustainability.

The most important problems in the two economies are also similar mainly the agrarian crisis and the need to generate more employment. In both economies, the social sectors have been neglected recently by public intervention. In both countries, the policy message appears to be the same, that the most basic issues are those that require to be addressed first, and if so, the other areas of expansion will probably look after themselves.

India has individual liberty, political pluralism, and the institutional framework to take advantage of globalization. However it is constrained by mass poverty, lackadaisical government, growing fiscal problems, and a poor physical infrastructure. China has much less degrading poverty than India, which has more trade and investment links, while Chinese have a superior physical infrastructure. It is rapidly conforming to global behaviour patterns, and creating an internationally accepted legal system. However it too has fiscal problems, hidden in the banking system, and political risk.

China's industrial strength and infrastructure, and its vast pool of skilled labour, make it a natural choice for the manufacturing sector. India, on the other hand, with booming information technology sector and its huge reserves of English-speaking graduates, is a better option for outsourced service and technology development facilities. China has been favoured heavily by multinational corporations (MNCs) for manufacturing, with only limited business process outsourcing (BPO) activity coming in from Japanese and Korean firms. As opposed to the concentrated outsourced services and R&D facilities found in India, China is the hub of manufacturing.

As the WTO and TRIPS agreements progress, the export orientation of each country may cross into the present domain of the other due to drops in garment quota requirements and strengthening of the IPR culture.

The key strategies of Chinese reforms was to first effect a massive increase in incomes in the rural areas, and then meet the demand for consumer goods by encouraging the growth of VTEs (Village and Town Enterprises). The VTEs met the demand for basic consumer goods in the rural areas itself. There was continuous decentralisation, and a system of profit taking with punishment for default. In India, the agricultural sector still accounts for about 70% of employment, but its share in GDP is down to 25% in other words the relative per capita income of the agricultural worker must be going down.

China can assist India in her globalization efforts, by cheaper imports from China and using them to produce low cost products in India itself, through the joint-venture strategy. By trading with China, India can be a little more competitive in global markets. A strategy of engagement with China and facing up to competition can be India's policy for the future.

India must emulate China by taking advantage of its cheap, hardworking and skilled workers to leverage better in world markets. To compete effectively, India needs to expand its primary and secondary education, and give more emphasis to vocational education and training.

China is infact "*many small markets*", rather than "*the world's biggest market*". China today has good infrastructure-railways, roads and airports-so there is for the first time substantial inter-city and inter-provincial commerce, as one city can compete against "backward manufacturers" in another. Consequently there is the rise of national domestic brands.

At the political level, the Communist Party of China, eaten underneath by corruption still survives. One day new attitudes will push aside the corruption of the old, and a new China will emerge. Beijing strikes hard against recalcitrant elements and dissidents-but dissidents can be muzzled-not their ideas.

Since 1978, when the great modernizer, Deng Xiao Ping began China's reforms, and later in the nineties with former President's Jiang Zemin's vision, China has moved rapidly in its growth rates. However the new Chinese leadership needs to move ahead faster in political reforms. To recall, Chairman Mao's words "*it takes only one spark to start a prairie fire*". The next spark should not cause any dramatic upheavals.

The share of manufacturing in China's GDP is 49%, and Services constitute 33% of GDP.The biggest current draw for international investors is the *"Western Development Project"* (headquarters in Chonqing), initiating grandiose plans for Xinjiang and Tibet.

At the geo-political level, Sino-Indian relations should rise above the present border disputes, and past tilts. Relations should be non-hyphenated, and stand-alone, not guided by any third country. India occupies a special place, as the land of the Buddha in China.There is also admiration in India for China's economic achievements. India has an edge over China in terms of intellectual capital for the future knowledge economy.

Some of the general strengths and weaknesses of India and China are enumerated below.

Strengths of China

- Confucian ethic of discipline and obedience.
- Authoritarian Militarist State, with severe penalties for non-compliance.
- Highly disciplined top leadership that implements decisions once agreed, without further argument.

- Productivity of Chinese labour is five times that of India.
- China has a system of incentives and disincentives at Central, State and Town-level for performance.
- Small-scale imitator of well-known brands, giving better quality for a lesser price, not the original branded manufacturer. Chinese "under design" products to make them affordable by poorer households. Those who can afford to pay more for superior quality do so. In India, established manufacturers are unlike the Chinese; they are conditioned by MNCs, whose practices evolved in markets that can afford high prices for superior products, and that suited an economy where capacities were restricted by license. China dominates export of labour-intensive products world-wide-India does not, except in gems and jewellery. Chinese manufactured goods exports as a % of GDP was 18%-as against 4% for India (1999-2000).
- China has a system of incentives and disincentives at central, state and town level- for performance and non-performance.
- Foreign investment in China is in land, buildings, plant and machinery. Of the comparatively small foreign investment in India, a high proportion is in portfolio investment, and in buying existing capacities.

Weaknesses of China

- Communist Party of China still dominating, with no democratic dissent tolerated.
- The Chinese legal system has still many weaknesses for corporate grievance redressal.
- China has yet to adapt fully to rules and regulations of a free market economy.
- China has lax labour regulations, and workers in many industries have to toil for longer hours.
- Working conditions are tough, as workers stay in crammed dormitories inside industrial zones to work from 8 A.M to 8

P.M.They are not allowed to form their own associations at national or regional level. This advantage may not last long, as workers become conscious of their rights. Even though labour issues are not raised at WTO, such unsound procedures and practices could come under attack.

- China's entry into WTO will call for a "fresh look" at its global interaction and domestic re-structuring.
- Corporate governance too is not of a high quality, as transactions are not wholly transparent. Managers of State Enterprises indulge in various irregularities-like siphoning of funds offshore, which in many cases comes back disguised as FDI.
- Chinese capital markets too are underdeveloped-regulations are not in tune with free-market earnings. Foreign investors can invest in B-group shares-only at Shanghai and Shenzen- and cannot indulge in A-group shares-meant strictly for locals.

Strengths of India

- A stable and vibrant democracy. *India's greatest achievement is sustaining a democracy in exceptionally difficult circumstances.*
- Wide use of the English Language.
- Availability of world-class scientific, technical, managerial and professional manpower.
- Established Western style corporate democracy and a functioning legal system for grievance redressal and contract enforcement.
- A growing and sizable middle-class estimated at 200 million.
- Our culture encourages risk without reward, and as our defence forces have shown, we can be extremely disciplined and productive.

Weaknesses of India

- Hypocrisy of our political leadership.
- Poor implementation capacity of our administration.
- Speculative mentality of our industry.

- Rampant corruption, stifling the delivery system of any constructive programme.
- *"Vested Interests" and "Entrenched Rural Hierarchies" hampering any societal changes.*
- Our bureaucrats and politicians have yet to develop awareness that more trade and intensified economic relations enhances India's security, power and influence.

The similarities are striking. China and India are amongst the five biggest countries in the world in terms of area, geographical diversity, population, market-size and economy measured in terms of purchasing power parity. Both countries were colonized by western powers, and attained independence within a few years of each other in the mid twentieth century. They both pursued socialist models of development before opening up gradually, China from 1978, and India from 1991.China and India are presently the fastest growing major economies of the world, although the majority of the population continues to be dependent on agriculture. The state sector continues to dominate economic activity in both countries, with the role of private enterprise expanding fast. In both China and India rapid economic growth has widened regional economic disparities.

Both China and India face serious fiscal problems and ballooning domestic debt and contingent liabilities, needing major public sector adjustments in the foreseeable future. However, much of India's public sector deficit has been absorbed directly by the government, whereas China has relied more heavily on the banking system to fund the deficit. Therefore, while India has higher fiscal deficits, China's banking system has more non-performing assets.

Corruption is endemic in both China and India.However, in China it is more centralized around the entrenched communist party, which practically guarantees quick action. In India corruption is more dispersed, and outcomes less certain. Because corruption in India is subject to legislative, media and judicial oversight, it is less of a systemic risk than in China.

China has shown far grater urgency in privatizing and closing a large number of state enterprises, while India's privatization progamme has floundered. While China has effectively lowered trade barriers, with customs tariff collections comprising only about 3%

ad valorem, Indian tariffs are still amongst the world's highest. Economic decentralization has proceeded at a much faster pace in China, with local governments in China having effective economic strengths and decision-making powers; wheras India's centralized economic control is loosening only gradually.

While China is a closed society run by a tightly knit communist party, India is an open, democratic society, with an independent judiciary and press. With political dissent not aired in the public domain, China has overt political stability, arguably difficult to sustain during a severe economic downswing.

Both China and India face major future developmental threats: for India these centre on policies to enhance savings and growth rates to remove poverty within a targeted time frame; for China the threats are more institutional, with institutions, especially financial, legal and political, not in sync with the needs of a market economy.

The areas of convergence of interest between China and India and the time-frame in which they start influencing decision making is given in the Table-2 below—

Table 2 : Areas of Convergence of Interest Between China and India

Area of Convergence	*When Became Apparent*	*Joint Approach*
Himalayan environment	First decade of the 21st Century	Joint eco-restoration in border areas and Tibet
Further Eastward or Southward expansion of NATO	First decade of the 21st Century	Commonality of interest with Russia
Any Further Weakening of Russia	Immediate	Several Possibilities
Increasing US military presence in Central Russia	Immediate	Commonality of interest with Russia
Asian Stability	Immediate	Several Possibilities
Global Multi-Polar Stability	Anytime in future	In concert with UN

Source: "Dealing with China in the 21st Century" in Restructuring South Asian Security by Vinod Saighal (cited in References)

China could overtake India as the next Information Technology (IT) power and business-outsourcing hub for countries like the US, despite its lack of experience. China's offshore services will mature within the next five years, and companies should begin looking at the country as a potential source for IT-enabled services. Lower costs (roughly 1/6th of US counterparts), political stability, strong GDP growth (7.9% in 2001)-the country offers the kind of environment needed by interested global companies.

India-China bilateral trade has now crossed the $12 billion mark. However, the top five exports to China comprise mainly primary or low value –addition products -iron- ore, plastic and linoleum, ores and minerals, marine products and drugs and pharmaceuticals. Her imports from China are electronic goods, coal, coke, and organic chemicals, silk, medicinal and pharmaceutical products. India should move up the value chain, and export more IT-related products and pharmaceuticals, as it is doing recently.

However, despite China's better image abroad, *the image of Indians abroad is very high in complete contrast the image of India is poor-but improving.* The *Indian diaspora* has gained considerable salience abroad, a number of Indian $ billionaires live in the US and are highly rated. Despite loud proclamations, foreign investors consider everything unfriendly about India-the government, the bureaucracy and the infrastructure. We have to change the mind-set and working of Indian institutions.

India's trade with China is set to grow to $20 billion by 2007. During 2005-06, trade between the two countries is expected to be around $15 billion. Trade and economic co-operation hold the key to strengthening overall bilateral relationship. During 2000-01, India-China trade volume was just $2 billion, but rose sharply to $11.3 billion in 2004-05.However, the trade basket needs diversification, from raw materials and products of natural resource-based industries. If the trade and economic linkages is to expand exponentially, it is imperative that diversification takes place in the commodity-mix. China and India between themselves produce practically everything, cheaply and with high quality.With high export growth rates-India and China is galloping, but they must also gallop in tandem with each other.

A recent study by Goldman Sachs shows that India will take a long time to catch up with China-may not catch up even by 2050.This is because China has a much larger base in GDP than India; therefore, even smaller relative increases in income for China would mean a higher absolute increase than India. This is shown from Table-2 below.

Table 3 : What will it take for India to catch up with China?

India	*Year*	*Growth Rate (%)*
To catch up China by	2050	8.9
To catch up China by	2020	11.6
Average growth rate since	2000	6.2
Average growth rate in	1990s	5.6
Average growth rate in	1980s	5.6

Source: Will India Catch-up with China? Mohan Guruswamy et al, Centre for Policy Alternatives, New Delhi.

China is today the world's manufacturing hub. India should emerge as the world's technology and IT (Information Technology) hub, if it follows pro-active policies. India and China thus have a lot to learn from each other's experience, and can be dynamic partners, rather than competitors in the globalised world.

REFERENCES

1. Chang, Gordon G *The Coming Collapse of China*, Random House, New York, 2001.
2. Gary S.Baker, *Chug Along with China*, ET, 2003.
3. Jayati Ghosh, *Divergent Development Models*, Frontline, September 9, 2005.
4. Tony Nash, China *or India? -It's China & India*, Economic Times, May 11, 2005.
5. Shroff, Minoo R, *China's Remarkable Economic Growth-Some Lessons,* Forum of Free Enterprise, Mumbai, 2000.

6. Wadhva, Charan D, *Geo-Economic Positioning of India's Trade and Allied Relations: Perspectives on India's Experience with Regional Integration* in V. A Pai Panandiker and Ashis Nandy, Contemporary India, Tata McGraw Hill Publishing Company Ltd. New Delhi.

7. Saighal, Vinod, *Re-structuring South Asian Security*, Manas Publications, New Delhi, 2000.

8. Mohan Guruswamy et al, *Will India Catch-up with China?* Centre for Policy Alternatives, New Delhi, 2005.

9. Yasheng huang and Tarun Khanna, *Can India Overtake China?* Foreign Policy,July-August, 2003.

14

SAARC, INDIA AND SINGAPORE

India and Singapore can reap the synergies of the re-vitalised SAARC, after the coming into force of the SAFTA (South Asian Free Trade Agreement) from July 1, 2006, and the operationalisation of the CECA (Comprehensive Economic Cooperation Agreement) between India and Singapore from August 2005.

South Asia is home to around two billion out of six billion people on this planet. The South Asian region though one of the world's poorest can aspire to be a trillion dollar economy, with services and manufacturing accounting for a larger chunk of GDP, compared to manufacturing in the years to come. There is little progress in substantial intra-regional cooperation. Intra-SAARC trade has made little headway so far. In 2005, intra-SAARC trade (exports+imports) was 5.2% of the total trade of the region. India accounts for 71% of intra-SAARC exports (mainly to Bangladesh, Nepal and Sri Lanka). Bangladesh accounts for 36% of intra-SAARC imports, due to large imports from India. In the current global context of regionalism, SAFTA will attract wider global attention in view of the combined huge market size and the growth potential of the region in terms of available resources.

South Asia has multiple heterogeneities-namely geographical, economic, political and social. The region doesn't lack resources, but lacks initiatives for building complementarities. Even if India is a dominant economy in SAARC it makes tremendous economic sense to enter into cooperation with India. Since India is an emerging fast moving economy, the smaller countries can stand to benefit immensely by accessing the large domestic market of India. It should give them great opportunities for developing their economies, particularly agriculture and industry.

If India invests in gas-based projects in Bangladesh, and later imports gas from that country, it will be much more meaningful in a South Asian context. Apart from trade, there will be the larger "peace and stability dividend", harmony and a more conducive environment for investment, employment, and effective resource mobilisation and utilisation for all countries. India has conferred the MFN (Most Favoured Nation) status on Pakistan for the purpose of trade, but Pakistan has been dragging her feet on conferring similar status to India on the plea that pending resolution of the "Kashmir issue", full fledged commercial cooperation with India is unviable. However Pakistan has recently "agreed" to extend SAFTA to India. It is hoped that with the operationalisation of SAFTA, new commodities will be extended to the trade basket.

The CECA (Comprehensive Economic Cooperation Agreement) with Singapore is India's first comprehensive economic cooperation Agreement with any country, and a role-model for India's Economic Agreements with other countries. This has been made possible by virtue of the strong bilateral relationship that India and Singapore have built over the years". Prime Minister Lee Hsien Loong, in a recent speech in New Delhi in July 2005, noted:"… India's influence is being felt all over Southeast Asia. In Singapore alone, there are more than 1,500 Indian companies. Many are regional headquarters, some even overseeing operations in the Indian market. Thousands of Indian professionals work in Singapore in IT, financial services and other fields.Bollywood movies enjoy a strong following …the stage has been set for a burgeoning bilateral relationship between Singapore and India, and wider and deeper cooperation between India and Southeast Asia. With greater collaboration and integration between the people of both sides, and continued reforms by those in Government, we can look forward to a vibrant and dynamic future for Asia".

India and Singapore recently agreed to complete negotiations on mutual recognition agreements (MRAs), and finalise areas for more intensive economic cooperation.FDI in infrastructure and SEZs (Special Economic Zones) are stressed. The rigid clauses in the DTAA (Double Taxation Avoidance Agreements) with Singapore as contrasted with Mauritius, is also the principal reason for low investments from Singapore.

A possible future area of cooperation is a trilateral linkage between SAARC, INDIA and SINGAPORE.

India and Pakistan have agreed not to levy import duties of more than 5% on products traded within SAFTA.The other five SAARC countries have also agreed to reduce their import duties by between 0% and 5% within the next 10 years.SAFTA will be totally effective only by 2016. *Intra-regional trade volume among SAARC countries stands at $6 billion, or a mere 4.4% of the total trade of member states, worth $135 billion.* This is in contrast to intra-regional trade of 55% in the EU, 61% in NAFTA and 25% in ASEAN. *Pakistan's "positive list approach"* regarding items which could be imported from India is the biggest obstacle to normal direct trade relations with India. Even if Pakistan does not give full- MFN status to India, it is not economically rational, for Pakistan not to put on the positive-list goods that it at present imports from other countries. Such an arrangement would introduce an element of fair competition that will benefit the Pakistani consumer and importer. If SAFTA is implemented in letter and in spirit, bilaterally traded goods could be brought back into the Indo-Pak ambit. In the indirect (unofficial trade), estimated to be US $ 2.5 billion, higher transportation costs make many potential Pakistani commodity exports to India uneconomical. Transit-facilitation needs to also be implemented, if Peshawar becomes the hub of India's trade with Afghanistan and Central Asia.

15

INDIA AND SINGAPORE—DYNAMIC ECONOMIC PARTNERS

Introduction

The city-state of Singapore is strategically located at a critical intersection of international commerce, and in the geo-strategic vicinity of India and China. Singapore commands attention on the international stage as a dynamic economy, and according to Michael Leifer as an "exceptional state".

India's links with Southeast Asia go back centuries. India has left the imprint of its great civilization all over the region-in religion, culture, arts and literature. However, during the first four decades after India's independence, India turned inwards. Its priority was self-sufficiency rather than interdependence, and these historic linkages weakened. Today, India is once again opening up and rediscovering the region. It is attracting investments from all over the world, especially in IT (Information Technology).Outward investments from India have also been increasing. Its external trade has increased, and with Southeast Asia trade has multiplied six times in the last ten years. If the reforms continue, India's interests and influence in the region will continue to grow. India's "Look East" policy and economic liberalization efforts coincided with Singapore's regionalization strategy of investing in emerging economies, providing a common ground for cooperation. Singapore is a natural gateway for India to engage in the region, because of its historical ties and special friendship between the two countries.

There have been many high-level visits exchanged between the two countries, including Heads of State and Heads of Government visits. Bilateral agreements on avoidance of double taxation, cooperation in shipping, tourism, civil aviation, information technology and science and technology have been signed between India and Singapore.

Singapore also played a leading role in India becoming a member of the ARF (ASEAN Regional Forum) and the ASEAN+1 Summit. Among the ASEAN states Singapore has gone the farthest to improve both bilateral and Associational ties. India's former Prime Minister,P.V Narasimha Rao, in his path-breaking Singapore lecture of September 1994,which set in motion India's "Look East" policy said"… The Asia-Pacific could be the spring board for our leap into the global market place. I am happy to have had this opportunity to enunciate my belief in this vision of a new relationship between India and the Asia-Pacific from Singapore, which I consider the geographic and symbolic centre of the Asia-Pacific". Since then, Singapore has been the key country for India's engagement with Southeast Asia. It was the country coordinator for the ASEAN-India dialogue. Singapore's exertions on behalf of India are openly acknowledged by the Indian policy making community.

During his visit to Singapore in August 2003, the then Indian External Affairs Minister candidly noted: "… in the development of our ties with ASEAN, few countries have been as creative and pro-active as Singapore. We are grateful to our many friends here, in particular, (then) Prime Minister Goh Chok Tong, for his vision and leadership in bringing India and ASEAN closer.

This has been made possible by virtue of the strong bilateral relationship that India and Singapore have built over the years". Prime Minister Lee Hsien Loong, in a recent speech in New Delhi in July 2005, noted:"… India's influence is being felt all over Southeast Asia. In Singapore alone, there are more than 1,500 Indian companies. Many are regional headquarters, some even overseeing operations in the Indian market. Thousands of Indian professionals work in Singapore in IT, financial services and other fields.Bollywood movies enjoy a strong following …the stage has been set for a burgeoning bilateral relationship between Singapore and India, and wider and deeper cooperation between India and Southeast Asia. With greater collaboration and integration between the people of both sides, and continued reforms by those in Government, we can look forward to a vibrant and dynamic future for Asia".

The increasingly close relations between India and Singapore in recent years have been underpinned by a dramatic growth in bilateral trade and investment links. The major items of Indian exports to Singapore are textile manufactures including apparel and yarn, precious stones and pearls, parts for office and data machines, aluminum, electrical machinery, fish and fish products and fruits and vegetables. The major items of India's imports from Singapore have been petroleum products, machinery, metallic ores/scrap, organic chemicals, primary plastics and scientific instruments. Singapore's economy complements India's economy, and does not threaten India's sensitive sectors. Singapore-India trade (US$7bn) is already half of total ASEAN-India trade (US $15bn).Singapore can therefore play a useful role as a pathfinder for India.

The recently concluded CECA(Comprehensive Economic Cooperation Agreement) between India and Singapore creates the necessary conducive environment for a strong bilateral relationship, and wider cooperation between India and Southeast Asia.CECA combines liberalized commercial transactions in goods and services, with two-way investment flows in untapped areas. It is a very big psychological step for India, signifying a new direction in India's economic diplomacy. It is India's first overarching economic pact with any country. Integral to the CECA is a wide array of established practices and proposed initiatives, ranging from dispute settlement arrangements and a review mechanism to an updated avoidance of double-taxation and other measures. India through the CECA has moved from the old policy of substantial self sufficiency to one where it wants to link up and open up markets in a controlled sort of way, and encourage linkages and exchanges. The CECA lays the groundwork for agreements with many other countries.

With an investment of $1.29 billion, Singapore has emerged as the third largest foreign investor in the country. The major investments in India from Singapore are channelised through three major agencies-Government of Singapore Investment Corporation, Monetary Authority of Singapore and Temasak Holdings. Many Indian companies, mainly trading and software companies have set up joint ventures and subsidiaries in Singapore to promote their business activities in the region, covering diverse product areas such as automobile ancillaries, precision tooling, palm kernel processing, micro and mini computers.

In the tourism sector, opportunities are emerging rapidly for Singapore as Indian tourists have become the highest spenders among the tourists to Singapore, and the fourth largest revenue generating market, with growing affluence among the Indian middle class. In the logistics sector, the Port of Singapore Authority (PSA) has been involved in port development and management in Tuticorin in Tamil Nadu and Piparav in Gujarat. These developments have the potential to lead to major investment opportunities for other Singapore firms in the logistics sector.

Defence- related research could be an area of future cooperation. Incremental interactions have taken place across a wide spectrum, ranging from education and culture. Singapore is also keen that India plays an appropriate role in a "creative fashion" in the maintenance of security along the Straits of Malacca.

The Economy

A former colonial trading port, serving the regional economies of maritime Southeast Asia, Singapore aspired to be a "global city" serving world markets and major multinational corporations. A quarter century after independence in 1965, the city-state had become a manufacturing center with one of the highest incomes in the region. As one of Asia's four "little dragons" or newly industrializing economies, Singapore along with the Republic of Korea (South Korea), Taiwan, and Hong Kong was characterized by an export-oriented economy, relatively equitable income distribution, trade surpluses with the United States and other developed countries, and a common heritage of Chinese civilization and Confucian values. The small island had no resources other than its strategic location and the skills of its nearly 2.7 million people. It has claimed a set of economic superlatives in the 1980s, including the world's busiest port, the world's highest rate of annual economic growth (11 percent), and the world's highest savings rate (42 percent of income).

Singapore has lived by international trade, as it had since its founding in 1819, and operated as a free port with free markets. Its small population and dependence on international markets meant that regional and world markets were larger than domestic markets, which presented both business managers and government policymakers with distinctive economic challenges and opportunities. The value of Singapore's international trade was more than three times its gross domestic product (GDP). The country's year-to-year economic performance fluctuated unpredictably with the cycles of world markets, which were beyond the control or even the influence of Singapore's leaders. In periods of growing international trade, such as the 1970s, Singapore could reap great gains, but even relatively minor downturns in world trade could produce deep recession in the Singapore economy, as happened in 1985-86. The country's dependence on and vulnerability to international markets shaped the economic strategies of Singapore's leaders.

The economy rests on five major sectors: the regional entrepôt trade; export-oriented manufacturing; petroleum refining and shipping; production of goods and services for the domestic economy; and the provision of specialized services for the international market, such as banking and finance, telecommunications, and tourism. The spectacular growth of manufacturing in the 1970s and 1980s had a major impact on the economy and the society, but tended to obscure what carried over from the economic structure of the past. Singapore's economy always depended on international trade and on the sale of services. An entrepôt was essentially a provider of services such as wholesaling, warehousing, sorting and processing, credit, currency exchange, risk management, ship repair and provisioning, business information, and the adjudication of commercial disputes. In this perspective, which focused on exchange and processing, the 1980s assembly of electronic components and manufacture of precision optical instruments were evolutionary steps from the nineteenth century sorting and grading of pepper and rubber. Both processes used the skills of Singaporeans to add value to commodities that were produced elsewhere and destined for consumption outside the city-state.

The dependence on external markets and suppliers pushed Singapore toward economic openness, free trade, and free markets. In the 1980s, Singapore was a free port with only a few revenue tariffs and a small set of protective tariffs scheduled for abolition in the 1990s. It had no foreign exchange controls or domestic price controls. There were no controls on private enterprise or investment, nor any limitations on profit remittance or repatriation of capital.

Foreign corporations were welcome, foreign investment was solicited, and fully 70 percent of the investment in manufacturing was foreign. The government provided foreign and domestic enterprises with a high-quality infrastructure, efficient and graft-free administration, and a sympathetic concern for the problems of businesses.

The vulnerability inherent in heavy dependence on outside markets impelled Singapore's leaders to buffer their country's response to perturbations in world markets and to take advantage of their country's ability to respond to changing economic conditions. Unable to control so much that affected their nation's prosperity, they concentrated on those domestic institutions that could be controlled. The consequence was an economy characterized by a seemingly paradoxical adherence to free trade and free markets in combination with a dominant government role in macroeconomic management and government control of major factors of production such as land, labor, and capital. The extraordinarily high domestic savings rate provided reserves to weather such economic storms as trade recessions and generated a pool of domestically controlled capital that could be invested to serve the long-term interests of Singapore rather than of foreign corporations.

The high savings rate, however, was the result of carefully formulated government programs, which included a compulsory contribution of up to 25 percent of all salaries to a government-controlled pension fund. The government held about 75 percent of the country's land, was the largest single employer, controlled the level of wages, and housed about 88 percent of the population in largely self-owned apartments. It also operated a set of wholly-owned government enterprises and held stock in additional domestic and foreign firms. Government leaders, deeply aware of Singapore's need to sell its services in a competitive international market, continually stressed the necessity for the citizens to master high levels of skills and to subordinate their personal wishes to the good of the community. The combination of devotion to free-market principles and the need for internal control and discipline in order to adapt to the demands of markets reminded observers of many family firms, and residents of the country commonly referred to it as Singapore Inc.

With a limited domestic market and almost no natural resources, Singapore was forced to integrate into the global economy early in its development. When Singapore separated from Malaysia, it lost its hinterland. It had no choice but to swiftly shift to an export-driven industrialization policy, slashing trade barriers and actively seeking foreign investment. This change in orientation brought Singapore an average growth rate of 10% from 1965 to 1979.In 1965,when Singapore first became independent, its total trade amounted to S$6.8 billion.Today,Singapore is the fifteenth largest trading nation in the world with its total merchandise trade in 2004 amounting to S$580 billion, three times Singapore's GDP.It has grown from a third world country, and the continued rapid economic development over the past years owes much to its open trade regime, clearly directed economic management and its position in the centre of a dynamic regional market. Political stability and a well developed infrastructure combine with very high rates of savings and investment, and attractive investment incentives have contributed to make the economy one of the strongest in the world.

Singapore has a highly industrialized economy. Agriculture and mining are of little importance. Their contribution to GDP is close to zero. 90% of food consumed in Singapore is imported. Financial and business services and manufacturing are the most important sectors accounting for 26.9% and 27.2% of GDP respectively. The most important manufacturing sector is electronics directly accounting for 52.5% of manufacturing export.

By tapping into the global grid of trade,investments,and capital, Singapore recorded an average annual growth rate of 7.3% and the nominal value of its non-oil domestic exports have grown by an average of 12% per annum.Singapore's trade to GDP ratio is the highest in the world. The importance of trade to Singapore is illustrated by the fact that since 1999, Singapore's total trade in goods and services has accounted on average for nearly 360% of GDP.Singapore is thus an advocate of the multilateral trading system as free trade has been crucial for its survival.

Singapore's sound macroeconomic policies, coupled with its openness helped it to recover rapidly from the effects of the Asian financial crisis. The Singapore economy recovered in 1999 and 2000 to register GDP growth of 6.9% and 9.7% respectively. This growth was fuelled by growth in IT spending as a result of the dot.com boom.

Singapore's key Economic Statistics is given in the Table-1 below—

Table 1 : Key Indicators of Singapore

GDP:	Purchasing power parity - $109.4 billion (2004 est.)
GDP - real growth rate:	1.1% (2004 est.)
GDP - per capita:	Purchasing power parity - $23,700 (2004 est.)
GDP - composition by sector:	Agriculture: negligible industry: 32.2% services: 67.8% (2004 est.)
Investment (gross fixed):	24.9% of GDP (2004 est.)
Inflation rate (consumer prices):	0.5% (2004 est.)
Labor force:	2.2 million (2004 est.)

Labor force - by occupation:	manufacturing 18%, construction 6%, transportation and communication 11%, financial, business, and other services 49%, other 16% (2003)
Unemployment rate:	4.8% (2004 est.)
Budget:	Revenues: $14.15 billion expenditures: $15.61 billion, including capital expenditures of $5.6 billion (2004 est.)
Public debt:	106.4% of GDP (2004 est.)
Agriculture - products:	rubber, copra, fruit, orchids, vegetables, poultry, eggs, fish, ornamental fish
Industries:	electronics, chemicals, financial services, oil drilling equipment, petroleum refining, rubber processing and rubber products, processed food and beverages, ship repair, offshore platform construction, life sciences, entrepot trade
Industrial production growth rate:	2.8% (2004 est.)
Electricity – production: 30.48 billion kWh (2001)	
Electricity - consumption:	28.35 billion kWh (2001)
Oil - consumption:	700,000 bbl/day (2001 est.)
Natural gas - consumption:	2.5 billion cu m (2001 est.)
Natural gas - imports:	2.5 billion cu m : Note: from Indonesia and Malaysia (2001 est.)
Current account balance:	$26.15 billion (2004 est.)
Exports:	$142.4 billion f.o.b. (2004 est.)
Exports - commodities:	machinery and equipment (including electronics), consumer goods, chemicals, mineral fuels
Exports - partners:	Malaysia 15.8%, US 14.3%, Hong Kong 10%, China 7%, Japan 6.7%, Taiwan 4.7%, Thailand 4.3%, South Korea 4.2% (2003)

Imports:	$121.6 billion (2003 est.)
Imports - commodities:	Machinery and equipment, mineral fuels, chemicals, foodstuffs
Imports - partners:	Malaysia 16.8%, US 14.1%, Japan 12%, China 8.7%, Taiwan 5.1%, Thailand 4.3% (2003)
Reserves of foreign exchange & gold:	$95.75 billion (2004 est.)
Debt - external:	$15.06 billion (2004 est.)
Economic aid - recipient:	NA
Currency:	Singapore dollar (SGD)
Currency code:	SGD
Exchange rates:	Singapore dollars per US dollar - 1.7422 (2003), 1.7906 (2002), 1.7917 (2001), 1.724 (2000), 1.695 (1999)
Fiscal year:	1 April - 31 March

Source: CIA Factbook-Singapore Statistics, 2005.

Thus, Singapore is a small economy accounting for only 1.2% of East Asia's GDP and 0.3% of world GDP.Its economy is however, highly dependent on external demands. Manufacturing, together with services, make up Singapore's twin engines of growth. The manufacturing sector accounted for 26.3% of Singapore's GDP, whilst services accounted for 63% of GDP in 2003.The services sector is a major employer, accounting for 75% of total employment. Agriculture is of very limited significance to the Singapore economy. The sector contributes less than 0.1% of Singapore's GDP.Only about 2% of the land area is used for agricultural purposes.

Trade Performance and Policy Options

Singapore's external trade pattern reflects the conditions in the external environment. Total trade recovered in 1999 as external conditions improved after the Asian financial crisis. Following a 22.9%expansion in 2000, Singapore's external trade contracted sharply by 9.4% during the 2001 recession. It has, however, stayed positive since 2002, with a 9.6% expansion in 2003, and an exceptionally strong growth of 22.5% in 2004, largely due to the rebound in global electronics demand, increase in pharmaceutical exports and pick up in demand from key markets. Malaysia, the US, EU, Japan, and China were Singapore's top five trading partners, accounting for 59% of total trade in 2004.Singapore's main exports and imports are electronics, oil and chemicals.

Singapore's total trade in services increased steadily from 51% of GDP in 1998 to approximately 63% in 2003.Its major trading partners in trade in commercial services are the US,EU,Japan,and the regional developing economies. The top ten trading partners accounted for more than three-fourths of Singapore's trade in services in 2003.The geographical pattern of Singapore's trade in services is thus broadly similar to trade in goods.

Singapore's export of services can be broadly divided into traditional transportation and travel services and the emerging trade-related financial, business, and technical services. Although the export of services grew at an annual rate of 9.4% during the period 1998-2002, it slowed down to 2.8% and 2.9% in 2001 and 2002 respectively. The two most important components of services imports were transportation and travel. Imports of services recorded an annual growth of 11% during 1998-2002, though it slowed down during the 2001-03 period amidst a deteriorating labour market, high retrenchments, and the occurrence of SARS.

Singapore's trade policy directions are underpinned by several factors—

- Constraints of a small domestic market with limited natural resources.
- Its dependence on the global economy; Singapore's economy is plugged into the international grid and cannot be insulated from key global trends. It is vulnerable to developments around the world.
- Its dependence on free access to markets around the world for its economic survival and growth.

The stated objectives of Singapore's trade policies are: to contribute towards the strengthening of a free, open and stable multilateral trading system; to develop Singapore into an international trading centre; to identify new markets while maintaining existing markets; to safeguard and diversify sources of imports; and to increase services exports. In general, Singapore maintains one of the most liberal trading regimes in the world. It has very few trade barriers and provides a favourable climate for trade cooperation for countries both in the immediate vicinity and beyond. It primarily follows a free trade policy.

Singapore's prosperity is thus inextricably linked to that of the region and the world. To secure and expand its political and economic space, Singapore has adopted a multi-pronged approach in pursuing trade liberalization initiatives through the multilateral trading system, bilateral free trade agreements (FTAs), regional trading arrangements (RTAs), and through regional groupings such as ASEAN, APEC, and ASEM (Asia-Europe Meeting).

Singapore needs to ensure that it remains integrated with the rest of the world through deeper multilateral, regional, and bilateral links. In light of these challenges, Singapore's policy is to continue to promote greater integration at the multilateral, regional, and bilateral levels. It will continue to adopt a multi-pronged approach to trade policy by engaging in bilateral and regional FTA negotiations. It will continue to play a proactive role at the WTO to keep the momentum of multilateral trade liberalization.

Investment Climate and Policies

Singapore is located at the heart of Southeast Asia which is a resource rich region with a market potential of some 300 million people. Thus, Singapore is well placed to serve the fast growing markets of this region. Singapore's unique location and sophisticated telecommunications network allow financial institutions and other companies in the country to transact business with any part of the world within the same working day.

Singapore has first-class infrastructure in telecommunications and transport particularly in sea and air. Singapore's Changi Airport has the most air-links in the Asia-Pacific.

Singapore has seven Free Trade Zones (FTZs), six for sea-borne cargo and one for air cargo within which a wide range of facilities and services are provided for storage and re-export of dutiable and controlled goods. Goods can be stored within the zones without any customs documentation until they are released in the market. They can also be processed and re-exported with minimum customs formalities. The FTZs at the port facilitate entrepot trade and promote the handling of transshipment cargo.They offer free 72-hour storage for import/re-export cargo.

The Economic Development Board (EDB) promotes foreign investments with a border-less view beyond Singapore and into the region. As Singapore's investment architect, it helps foreign as well as local companies plan global business strategies and configure their activities from their base in Singapore. The EDB adds value to investors by providing a one-stop investment promotion service to identify business opportunities in Singapore and the region, and helps them set up their operations speedily.

Singapore's regulatory environment is business-friendly and is characterized by transparency and clarity. The bureaucracy is generally considered to be efficient and effective. Prior to implementing any law or regulation, the government usually consults relevant bodies and agencies, companies and the public. Various rules and regulations relating to tax,labour,banking,finance,industrial health and safety,arbitration,wages and training are formulated and reviewed with the interests of foreign investors and local enterprises in mind.However,local laws give regulatory bodies wide discretion to modify and impose new conditions. This allows government agencies to negotiate the way they provide incentives or other services to foreign companies on a case-by-case basis.

Singapore has a highly open investment regime, through which it seeks to overcome land and labour constraints. It aims to progress into the league of developed countries by attracting firms that can build up the country's technological base and labour force capabilities.Moreover,attracting foreign investment into the country has been an economic strategy of the government since independence.Consequently, the country's legal framework and public policies have always been investor-friendly.

The government of Singapore generally does not restrict or discourage foreign investment either to protect local industries or for any other reasons. However, restrictions on investment in a limited number of sectors exist. Armament manufacturing is strictly closed to foreign investment. Other sectors where foreign investments are limited include news media, telecommunications, broadcasting and domestic banking.Moreover; there can be no foreign ownership of public utility services.

Incentives are used both for the promotion of new investments in industries and services and for encouraging existing companies to upgrade through mechanization and automation and through the introduction of new products and services.

India-ASEAN Relations

India has moved purposefully in developing a broad economic and strategic partnership with the dynamic countries of South East Asia.

In pursuance of India's "Look East" policy, the dialogue has moved from a limited sectoral partnership (1992) to a full dialogue partnership (1995) and membership of the high-profile strategic forum ARF (ASEAN Regional Forum) in 1996, culminating in ASEAN+ India summits since 2002.

A FTA (Free Trade Agreement) between India and ASEAN would come into being in 10 years, and India was committed to aligning its peak tariff to East Asian levels by 2007.

The highlights of the framework agreement lays down that negotiations on FTA in goods would begin in 2004,and be concluded by 2005. Talks on FTA in services as well as investments would start in 2005 and be concluded by 2007. Areas of economic co-operation would include trade facilitation measures, sectors of co-operation and trade and investment promotion measures. The framework agreement provides for exchange of tariff concessions on the "early harvest programme" (EHP). Concessions and differential treatment has been given to Cambodia, Laos, Myanmar and Vietnam, the lesser-developed members of ASEAN.

India's economic potential and geo-strategic importance in Southeast Asia in the post-cold war world is today recognised as an important aspect of international diplomacy. However, India needs to have a clearer "Focus" and even a "Vision" with regard to its ties with the ASEAN.

There is much scope for further expanding and deepening our cooperative agenda, synergizing the economies of India and ASEAN and exploring new avenues for diplomatic complementarities.

India-ASEAN cooperation has progressed substantially in many spheres-mainly in science and technology, IT and electronics, HRD, transport and infrastructure, space technology, tourism and trade and investment. These initiatives are however not adequately reflected in trade figures.

India also signed a landmark free-trade agreement with Thailand and four other accords for enhancing co-operation in agriculture, tourism and science. The FTA will provide a free-trade area in goods to begin by 2010, and in services and investment from 2006.

The Indo-ASEAN two-way trade grew by 30% from U.S $7.6 billion in 1999 to $ 16 billion in 2005. ASEAN-India trade is still at a very low level, accounting for only 1% of ASEAN's global trade in 2005, while India's trade to ASEAN countries still hovers around 9% of its global trade. The volume of trade is still small considering the vast potential for trade that exists among countries of over 1.5 billion people, and it is hoped the target of $30 billion will be reached by 2010.The list of goods for which duties are brought down to zero by 2007 include a host of petrochemicals and polyesters, apart from other items like marine foods, white goods, electrical machinery, precious stones, office equipment, printed circuits and key auto-components like gear box and petrol engines. The pact with Thailand is to be followed by a similar agreement with Singapore and ultimately the entire ASEAN region.

The level of investment flows on both sides has a lot of untapped potential and can easily rise to $ 2 billion by 2007, with sustained efforts by both sides. The redeeming fact is that there are substantial investments by both India and ASEAN in each other's countries.

Although there have been significant changes in commodity composition of India's trade with ASEAN countries in recent years, components of the trade basket could do with substantial revision, with an increasing emphasis on India moving up the value chain.

India should also intensify its marketing thrust to ASEAN countries to correct the asymmetry in trade relations. Both infrastructure and technology can be hawked much more aggressively. Our exporters should negotiate much harder, offer more competitive terms, adhere to delivery schedules, and provide effective after-sales service. A marketing culture among our exporters, combined with a bit of hard sell, could help India make decisive inroads into the ASEAN markets.

Intensive efforts to promote business synergies on the two sides in areas such as infrastructure, IT, biotechnology, and tourism got a positive boost with the India-ASEAN Business Summits.

A trade pact with ASEAN is the best beginning since India has traditionally enjoyed many links-economic and strategic- with the region, although there is a lot of untapped potential. However, there are major differences in "tariff rates" between India and the big five of ASEAN.Indian customs duties are on an average at least twice and in many cases thrice as high as in ASEAN.Thus tariff equalization and rationalization will not be easy for a free trade to appear in the near future. Moreover changes to domestic tariff and commercial policy will be difficult because it may hurt the interests of domestic producers.

We should also try to strengthen strategic alliances with the *guanxi (*overseas Chinese networks) who control most of the distribution channels in Malaysia, Singapore and to some extent Thailand.

India should also make available information on its capabilities in fields like IT, and market these better in countries like the Philippines and Brunei, as trade with these two ASEAN countries is virtually non-existent.

Possibilities for functional cooperation are limitless, and enthusiasm should translate into tangible gains. India also needs to deepen her links with MGC (Mekong Ganga Cooperative forum) - a new co-operative forum floated by India with five of its eastern neighbours-Myanmar, Thailand, Cambodia, Vietnam and Laos. Tourism, culture and education are given precedence. The terms of India-ASEAN engagement needs to be taken much more seriously. Transport, communications and infrastructure will be prioritised in the next phase. The MGC also provides immense opportunities for India's private sector to create a niche in the region; India can make up for its past mistakes. Indo-ASEAN cooperation in tourism, culture and education can also be strengthened in Indonesia and Malaysia.

ASEAN also faces the problem of disparity in development, the new entrants- Laos, Vietnam and Cambodia showing lower levels of performance compared to the other members-and will take time to integrate fully into the ASEAN framework. India can offer its help here as well by providing interest-free credit facilities for speedier development of these countries, and cashing in on the tremendous good-will that existed for her in the cold-war days.

There is also immense scope for further enhancing joint ventures in manufacturing, consultancy, leasing and trading outfits between India and ASEAN.

Other measures to promote greater India-ASEAN interaction should include relaxation of visa restrictions by ASEAN countries much more to facilitate greater collaboration among businessmen and technical personnel, opening up of the financial and banking sector, reduction of non-tariff barriers, sustained improvement in the delivery system of the Indian bureaucracy, and continuing to give explicit economic orientation to foreign policy.

While India's membership of ARF enables it to participate in regional security issues, we would seriously undermine our long term strategic and economic interests, if we do not take into account China's rapidly expanding economic and strategic profile in our eastern neighbourhood. While India's trade with ASEAN is currently around $16 billion annually, China's trade with ASEAN economies is multi-layered and currently stands at $ 60 billion.

Indo-ASEAN Trade and Investment

India's merchandise exports to ASEAN have more than tripled from about US$ 1.0 billion (5.7% of its world exports) to US$ 3.4 billion in 2001-02 (7.7% of its world exports).The overall trend has been upwards, except during the Asian crisis period of 1997-99.The rising trend of merchandise exports from India to ASEAN has been accompanied by a shift in the share of individual countries in India's total exports to ASEAN during this period. ASEAN countries are more important for India as import sources than as exports markets. Among ASEAN-members, Singapore and Malaysia have been India's prominent trading partners and India's trade with Laos has been the least in value terms. Growth in India's exports to ASEAN in recent years has been much higher in comparison with other important destinations. ASEAN's position in India's total trade relative to EU and North America has improved between 1991-92 and 2001-02. Shares of EU and North America in India's exports has been declining, whereas that of ASEAN has been on the rise.

India's aggregate balance of trade with ASEAN-5 shows that India posted deficits in every year since 1994, which became more pronounced in the last five years. This trend is attributed to the pattern to the relatively higher deficits with Singapore and Malaysia, and India's simultaneous inability to generate matching surplus elsewhere in the region even when the balance-of-trade is in its favour.

The share of ASEAN-5 in India's Global Exports and Imports is given in the Table-2 below-

Investment relations between ASEAN and India have remained rather limited. This is due to the fact that only Singapore, and to some extent, Malaysia has significant investments in India, and due to the limited capacity of Indian companies to invest abroad until recently. The share of ASEAN-6 in India's total approved FDI inflows increased nearly fourfold from 2% to about 8% between 1996 and 1998.Malaysia has made substantial investments in expanding capacities in selected infrastructural areas such as logistics and highways in India. It has also been cooperating to assist India in providing infrastructure expertise and investments in the energy sector, particularly for oil and gas exploration and in downstream processing activities.

Table 2 : Share of ASEAN-5 in India's Global Exports and Imports

	1991	*1996*	*2001*
Share in India's Global Exports (%)			
Indonesia	1.3	2.7	1.2
Malaysia	1.6	2.3	1.7
Singapore	2.3	3.1	2.5
Philippines	0.4	2.5	0.5
Thailand	5.2	2.0	1.5
Share in India's Global Imports (%)			
Indonesia	0.3	1.5	2.5
Malaysia	1.6	3.4	3.2
Singapore	5.1	5.7	5.6
Philippines	0.1	0.5	0.1
Thailand	0.3	0.7	1.0

Source: ASEAN Statistical Yearbook, ASEAN Secretariat.

The motivation for the current and future Indian investments abroad is economic efficiency and profitability criteria (pull factors), rather than to escape restrictive business environment at home (push factors). This is indicated by the fact that over the past few years, over 150 firms from India have located in Singapore, contributing to its economy and to employment generation. Indian companies are also poised to invest in Thailand (auto components sector), in Indonesia and Vietnam (motor vehicles and energy sector), and in the Philippines (ICT sector).These opportunities arise from substantial complementarities that exist between India and ASEAN in factor endowments, economic structure, skils and capabilities. The experience and competencies of Malaysia and Singapore in infrastructure development complements India's needs for physical infrastructure, particularly in the area of roads, industrial parks and housing estates.

India-Singapore Trade

Singapore is the largest market in ASEAN for India's merchandise exports, followed by Malaysia, Thailand, Indonesia, and the Philippines.

Singapore is India's largest trading and investment partners in ASEAN. The increasingly close relations between India and Singapore in recent years have been underpinned by a dramatic growth in bilateral trade and investment linkages. India is looking for infrastructure investments, critical technologies and export markets. Singapore has surplus capital and could be a useful partner in infrastructure development in India as well as investment in Indian companies.

Major items of India's Exports

The major items of India's exports to Singapore in 2005 were Crude petroleum, Refined Motor spirit, Petroleum oils, Polished diamonds for jewellery, Polished industrial diamonds, articles of Jewellery, Aluminum Unwrought, Aluminium sheets, Parts & accessories of computers, Synthetic fabrics, Silk fabrics, Embroidery/ Table linen of Man Made Fibres, Combed cotton, Knitted T-shirts, Vests, Benzene, Dyes, Acids, Insecticides, Fungicides, Household articles of stainless steel, Corrugated products of iron and steel, Forged/stamped articles of iron and steel, Bars and Rods of iron steel, Parts of Boring or Sinking machinery, X-ray tubes, Medical Surgical Dental or Veterinary instruments/ appliances, Penicillin, Rice, Sugar, Cashew nuts, Essential oil, Crabs live/dried, Fish (fresh/chilled/dried), Titanium ore, Menthol, Diesel/semi-diesel generating sets, Static converters, Valves/Taps Cocks for Pipes, Boilers, tanks etc, Bus/lorry tyres, Tobacco. These items in value terms constitute over 70% of India's exports to Singapore.

Major Items of India's Imports

The major items of India's imports from Singapore in 2005 were parts and accessories of Computers and Computer peripherals, Integrated Circuits, Cellular phones, CD ROMs, Styrene, P-Xylene, O-Xylene, Polypropylene, Vinyl Acetate, Topped Crudes, and Parts of boring and sinking machinery. Nickel, Tin (unwrought), lead (unwrought) Aluminium (unwrought) Zinc (unwrought), Waste & scrap of Iron and steel, Photographic chemicals, Sewing Machines, Ball/Roller bearings, Parts for bulldozers, Parts of Aero planes/ Helicopters, Parts for Audio/Video recorders, Medical instruments and appliances, parts of cellular phones, parts of motor vehicles, Cigarettes, pigments, Parts of Cathode Ray Tubes, Auto parts, parts for electrical Machines & apparatus. These items in value terms constitute over 60 % of India's imports from Singapore.

Total trade between India and Singapore has been steadily increasing since 1999. The trade between India and Singapore increased by 3.22% (in 2001), to S$ 6.88 billion, and decreased by 1.16% (in 2002). On comparing the trade figures of 2003 with 2002, it is seen that total trade has gone up by 16.20%. India's Imports from Singapore have increased by 14.22% and exports to Singapore by 21.25%. Over a period of 5 years India's imports from Singapore have increased by 26.88 %, whereas, during the same period India's exports to Singapore have increased by 100.8 %.Moreover, it may be noted that most of Singapore's exports to India consists of re-exports, which constitutes slightly over 50% of Singapore's exports to India. This is given in Table-3 below.

Table 3 : India-Singapore Trade

Year	*Singapore's Exports to India*		*Of Which Re-exports*		*Singapore's Imports from India*		*Total Trade*	
	(S$ bln)	*(US$bln)*	*(S$ bln)*	*(US$bln)*	*(S$ bln)*	*(US$bln)*	*(S$ bln)*	*(US$bln)*
1999	4.24	2.50	2.28	1.35	1.25	0.74	5.49	3.23
2000	4.80	2.74	2.71	1.54	1.86	1.06	6.66	3.81
2001	4.87	2.76	2.87	1.63	2.00	1.13	6.87	3.90
2002	4.71	2.67	2.79	1.58	2.08	1.18	6.79	3.85
2003	5.38	3.16	2.89	1.70	2.51	1.48	7.89	4.64

Balance of Trade

The balance of trade has remained in favour of Singapore since 1999. However despite growth in bilateral trade, the balance of trade in favour of Singapore has more or less remained same for the last five years in value terms (in S $). Indian exports to Singapore have been steadily increasing, growing in S$ terms by 48.8% (2000), 7.52% (2001) and 3.5% (2002), and 21.25% (2003).

Table 4 : Comparison of Trade Balance Between India and Singapore

(Value in S$ billion)	*1999*	*2000*	*2001*	*2002*	*2003*
India's Import from Singapore	4.24	4.80	4.84	4.72	5.38
India's Export to Singapore	1.25	1.86	2.00	2.07	2.51
Balance of Trade	-2.99	-2.94	-2.84	-2.65	-2.87

Investment Patterns

Singapore has emerged amongst the top foreign investors in India. During the period January 1991 to May 2003, approvals for Foreign Direct Investment from Singapore to India (excluding NRI and euro issues/portfolio investment) amounted to Rs.53 billion (approx USD 1.2 billion,) making Singapore among the largest foreign investors in India. Annual break-up since 1995 of Singapore's investment, and share of total FDI (excluding NRI and portfolio investment) in India, is given in Table-5 as follows:-

Table 5 : Approvals For Fdi In India

Year	*(in Rs. million) Total World FDI* (in Rs. Million)*	*Singapore FDI (in Rs. Million)*	*Singapore FDI as % of Total*
1995	301725	9910	3.28
1996	286923	3198	1.11
1997	485720	8619	1.77
1998	268392	7673	2.86
1999	246855	8259	3.35
2000	156183	3232	2.07
2001	203319	3799	1.87
2002	111398	3722	3.34
2003 (up to May)	17436	1254	7.2
Total (since 1991)	2,280399*	53604	2.35%

* (Excluding NRI/ Euro issues)

Source: SIA News Letter, June 2003

Singapore Investments

Some of the Government-Linked Corporations (GLCs) of Singapore's projects include Ascendas' Information Technology Park in Bangalore, the participation of the Port of Singapore Authority (PSA) in both equity (40%) and management of Piparav Port, Gujarat, PSA's 30-year contract for operation and management of the Tuticorin Port, Singtel's joint venture with Bharati Telecom and Singapore Technologies Telemedia's JV with ModiCorp. The Government of Singapore Investment Corporation (GIC) has registered itself in India as an Financial Institutional Investors, and has committed Rs. 119 million in HDFC Ltd. Apart from investing in other stocks and equities.

The GIC along with other investors has invested Rs.11 billion (S$407 million) for a 13.6 percent stake in India's ICICI Bank as its strategic partners. In Dec 03 Temasek holdings has acquired a 5.2% stake costing around S$342.2million in ICICI Bank. In January 04, Temasek Holdings, Singapore Government's investment arm, bought a stake in Matrix laboratories, Hyderabad for S$114.7million, thus getting a 14% equity stake in the company.

Singapore-based MNCs and Singapore's government-linked-companies (GLCs) such as Singapore Telecom, Port of Singapore Authority and Singapore Technologies have also made investments in India. Singapore's private sector companies have made small-scale investments in health care, real estate, and tourism.Favourable experience and profitability of Singapore's technology park in Bangalore has created a positive environment for investments by Singapore in India.

Singapore, through its government holding company, government of Singapore Investment Corporation (SGIC), is also one of the largest Foreign Institutional Investors in India. The majority of the MNCs in Singapore have used Mauritius to route investments to India because of its favourable double taxation treaty with India.Thus, the official figures of inflows of FDI from Singapore to India is understated as they exclude those investments routed via Mauritius.

Temasek and Stanchart Bank formed the Merlion - India Fund of US $ 100 million for investing in mid to late stage Indian Companies. The fund does not cover investment in infrastructure, real estate and trading. This fund was set up for the purpose of Singapore companies investing in Indian companies expanding in India and abroad. The fund has invested (in December 03) S $ 35 million to a 5.46% stake in Aurobindo Pharma, Hyderabad.

The Singapore Business Federation (SBF), which is the government-guided amalgamation of different chambers of commerce and industry, is also likely to open an office in India. Individual chambers of commerce associated with SBF such as the Chinese, Malay and Indian chambers might also open their own separate offices.

While Singapore's manufacturing base centering on electronics and petrochemicals, and its role as an entrepot centre will continue to sustain the merchandise trade, the emerging opportunities are largely in the services sector, particularly in the Information and Communication Technology (ICT), logistics services, business and financial services, tourism, and health services This is more so as Singapore plans to develop itself into a service hub and improve its capabilities in areas where there exist considerable complementarities with India. The opportunities are not only in trade in services transactions (such as used by Singapore Airlines of India as a base for some of its IT-enabled services) but also in investments (presence of Indian ICT, Pharmaceutical, and trading companies in Singapore, and Singapore's investments in India's ICT, tourism and health services, besides in port development and logistics). The probable involvement of Singapore's polytechnics in technical education in Tamil Nadu, and perhaps other states, could further strengthen bilateral linkages.

The Info-Comm. Development Authority of Singapore (IDA) has signed an MoU with India's premier IT training company, National Institute of Information Technology (NIIT) to persuade IT professionals to locate in Singapore, from anywhere in the world. As Indian professionals are internationally competitive and culturally compatible, India is among the largest sources of IT manpower in the world, a significant proportion is likely to be sourced from India. This could create a dynamic Indian Diaspora with positive externalities for both countries. The investments by Singapore Telecom (SingTel) in India's telecom sector in partnership with India's Bharti Televentures to take advantage of India's huge potential domestic telecom and Internet market is also another example in this sector.

In the tourism sector, opportunities are emerging rapidly for Singapore as Indian tourists have become the highest spenders among tourists to Singapore and became the fourth largest revenue generating market, with growing affluence among the Indian middle class. Singapore tourism authorities has also been actively involved in promoting select areas in India as a tourism destination for Singaporeans, through a joint marketing by the Government of India tourism office already established in Singapore.

Indeed, Singapore's two airlines, Singapore Airlines and Silk Air have quite liberal rights to fly to several destinations in India. They could however take greater advantage of India's open sky policies concerning air cargo. In the logistics sector, the Port of Singapore Authority (PSA) has been involved in port development and management in Tuticorin in Tamil Nadu and Piparav in Gujarat. These have the potential to lead to major investment opportunities for other Singapore firms in the logistics sector. Negotiations between Singapore's largest supermarket operator, NTUC Fairprice which has close links with the government, and India's Apollo Group, one of Asia's largest hospital and health-care management companies to set up a pharmacy and retail chain of convenience stores numbering in the hundreds in petrol stations run by the Indian oil corporation also hold promise for greater economic linkages. It would contribute to Singapore's food security, and to its supply chain for other essential household goods. Indian IT companies have recognized the importance of Singapore as a marketing and development center, and their presence is growing. As Indian businesses have been given much greater freedom to invest abroad, presence of Indian companies from other sectors in Singapore is also increasing. This should also have a positive impact on Singapore's importance as a business hub, and on trade in business services.

Singapore intends to increasingly rely at the margin on investment income from abroad. Its rather large reserves, conservatively estimated to be about US $ 90 billion, are mostly invested abroad through holding companies of the Singapore government. It is suggested that these holding companies consider passive investments in infrastructure projects in India. Setting up of a physical presence in India by the Singapore Government Investment Corporation (SGIC), and other such Singapore government investment companies, merits serious consideration. Currently, these holding companies do act in a limited way as venture capitalists for Indian IT companies. However, there is much greater scope in not only the IT sector but also in biotechnology, life sciences, and other areas. For these purposes also, physical presence in India would be beneficial.

India-Singapore CECA

On June 29, 2005, India and Singapore signed a Comprehensive Economic Co-operation Agreement (CECA), the first of its kind for India, concluding two years of intensive negotiations. Its distinctive feature is that it is indeed 'comprehensive' and covers trade in goods and services, investment flows and encompasses a double taxation avoidance agreement (DTAA).Such wide-ranging agreements are, in a sense, the logical next step in a world economy increasingly driven by the flows of trade in goods, services and movement of capital.

For, India, it seems, the gains driving the partnership with Singapore would be in the area of services exports and in-bound FDI.Singapore accounted for approximately 2.5% of India's FDI inflows from 1991 to 2005 and has been investing especially in Indian infrastructure industries such as ports, telecommunications and banks, in the last few years. The Singapore government has in the past indicated its willingness to set up a $1 billion fund to invest in India after the CECA comes into force. Since the island-nation is a free-trading port, most of the duties on its tariff lines are zero and there is much it can offer by way of tariff concessions, though the hope is that synergies in Indian manufacturing and Singaporean branding expertise can be tapped to profit in the ASEAN market. One of the difficult aspects of the negotiations was determining the rules of origin (ROO)-by which the nationality of goods are determined to ensure that only citizens of the contracting country avail of trade concessions-as there were concerns in India that exporters from third countries could use the Singapore route to dump cheap goods inn the country.

The Prime Minister of Singapore, Lee Hsien Loong, believes that the main advantage for Singapore from the agreement is tariff less access to the Indian market in a large number of goods. Besides some banks will have access to the Indian market. For the Indian side, the big gain from the agreement is on the movement of professionals. Also, inward investment into India from Singapore has become very attractive.

The CECA with Singapore is "a free trade agreement (FTA) plus", covers trade in goods as also services, besides investment flows and "mutual recognition"clauses, is expected to help Singapore widen its frontiers of international commerce. Singapore has close economic linkages with the US, Japan and China among others.

The business communities in both countries could now "leverage" on this win-win development.

In the services sector, Indian companies stand to benefit through increased market access in distribution services, including retail trading, business services, market research, legal, environmental management, management consultancy, tourism, real estate, consultancy and advertising, engineering, architecture and computer-related services.

India was Singapore's 14th largest trading partner in 2004/05 and bilateral trade has nearly tripled within the past decade, from S$4 billion in 1995 to S$11.8 billion in 2004/05. Over the last year, while negotiations were ongoing, bilateral trade with India increased by almost half, from S$7.8 billion in 2003, making India the fastest growing trading partner among the major economies.

The provisions of the CECA are broad, aiming not only to liberalise bilateral trade in goods and services but also to increase investment and ease visa regulations. The CECA is likely to enhance further Singapore's position as Asia's trade hub, boost Indian trade with East Asia, and encourage more foreign investment in India.

Under the provisions of the CECA, Singapore will cut all duties on goods made in India (excepting tobacco and automobiles), while India will remove or reduce duties on a range of Singaporean products, covering around four-fifths of its exports. As a first step India will scrap duties on 506 items immediately (from August 1st) and will phase out tariffs on a further 2,202 items over the next four years, also reducing duties on another 2,407 items by 2009. However, it will maintain the current level of duties on a list of 6,551 items from Singapore. The deal also includes agreements on trade in services and a commitment to liberalise visa requirements for professionals in 127 fields.

Trade Gains

Bilateral trade between the two countries is surging, rising over 50% in the fiscal year 2004/05 (April-March) to US$6.38bn, according to India's Ministry of Commerce and Industry. India's imports from Singapore were worth US$2.58bn in 2004/05, consisting principally of electronic goods (39% of its total imports from Singapore), organic chemicals (14%) and transport equipment (9%). India's exports to Singapore totalled US$3.80bn, consisting largely of crude oil and petroleum products (46% of its total exports to India), gems and jewellery (15%), and machinery and instruments (5%). India's bilateral trade surplus with Singapore in the last fiscal year was US$1.21bn.

Given the diversity of products and services that make up trade between India and Singapore, there is ample potential for the CECA to boost bilateral commerce significantly. India has been granted more or less complete duty-free access to Singapore, which is positioning itself (primarily through the negotiation of bilateral free-trade agreements, or FTAs) as Asia's trade hub. Singapore has signed FTAs with six other countries (including Japan, Australia and the US) and is negotiating with a further 12—a deal with South Korea is due to be concluded soon.

Thanks to Singapore's FTA network, India's exporters will have greater access to eastern Asian markets as a result of the CECA. Singapore is already India's largest trading partner in the Association of South-East Asian Nations (ASEAN), accounting for 37.5% of its trade with ASEAN members, but this is likely to grow. The CECA's provisions establishing common measures and standards for Singaporean and Indian goods will enable traders in Singapore to push Indian products more easily through the region.

India's trade policy is less clear cut than Singapore's, though. A broader strategy for establishing bilateral deals worldwide is hampered by domestic concerns about increased competition. Acknowledging complaints from Indian manufacturers about the threat of foreign competition, the CECA is hardly generous in terms of import liberalisation. As well as keeping tariffs unchanged on over 6,500 Singaporean products, India has negotiated the application of stringent rules-of-origin safeguards to prevent third-party goods reaching the Indian market via Singapore. A minimum of 40% of value must be added in Singapore for products to qualify for access under the CECA's tariff schedule—a stipulation similar to that which has caused friction in India's FTA negotiations with Thailand.

Despite its limitations, the deal with Singapore does mark a watershed in India's broader strategy of encouraging domestic economic growth through promoting export-oriented industries. It was significant that India's cabinet approved the deal just three days after the first meeting of the revamped Board of Trade, a collaborative government/industry forum in charge of developing a coherent national trade strategy. At this meeting the commerce and industry minister, Kamal Nath, exhorted the body to come up with ways to boost India's total trade to US$500bn in the next four years. (By comparison, India's trade in goods in 2004/05 was an estimated US$173bn.) With most of the rest of Asia committed to establishing free-trade networks, rather than relying on the World Trade Organisation, Mr. Nath presumably had deals like the CECA in mind as a first step to achieving this goal.

Investment Implications

The provisions of the CECA related to investment are equally as significant for India. As of December last year Singapore had invested US$6.41bn in India, making it the ninth-largest investor in the country. (According to the Indian commerce ministry, Singapore's investments in India grew 114% in fiscal 2004/05 from 2003/04.) The CECA is expected to boost this considerably. Singaporean institutional investments in Indian technology, manufacturing, financial services and aviation are to rise to US$5bn within the first year of the CECA's implementation, while Singaporean investment in India's infrastructure would top US$2bn.

Certainly, there are measures in the deal that will promote investment. For example, it revamps a bilateral double-taxation-avoidance treaty that was first signed in 1994 to give Singapore the same status as Mauritius (which had hitherto been unique in that its companies could invest in India without paying capital gains tax on profits earned there). The CECA provisions liberalising trade in financial and other services—paving the way for an air-services deal and an open-skies agreement, for example—are also likely to boost business between the two.

The CECA contains some important specific provisions regarding Singaporean investment. It allows the government-linked investment agencies Temasek Holdings and the Government of Singapore Investment Corp each to invest 10% stakes in Indian companies, whereas previously they had been restricted to acquiring 10% between them. Temasek alone has invested almost US$1.5bn in India in the past 18 months, with stakes in India's largest bank (ICICI), its largest healthcare firm (Apollo Hospitals Enterprises), Tata Consultancy Services, and an automotive firm, Mahindra & Mahindra. It is also one of India's foremost private equity investors.

The CECA also opens up India's financial services sector to Singaporean investment, allowing three banks from the city-state—DBS Holdings, Oversea-Chinese Banking Corp and United Overseas Banking—to set up branch operations in India. The three may either set up wholly owned subsidiaries (in which case they will be subject to local regulations) or set up regional branches, in which case they will be limited to opening

KEY PROVISIONS OF THE CECA*

Improved Avoidance of Double Taxation Agreement

An Avoidance of Double Taxation Agreement ("DTA") provides for avoidance of double taxation of income earned in one Contracting State by a resident of the other and makes clear the taxing rights between the two Contracting States on all forms of income from cross-border economic activities between the two Contracting States. The DTA thus helps to facilitate the flow of trade, investment, technical know-how and expertise between the two Contracting States by eliminating double taxation of income.

Singapore and India have agreed on a protocol to improve the existing DTA, which was signed in January 1994. The main improvement to the DTA is that tax residents will enjoy capital gains tax exemption on investments in India. However, a tax resident will not be entitled to the capital gains exemption if its affairs are arranged primarily to take advantage of the benefits of the DTA. In addition, a shell/conduit company with negligible or nil business operations or with no real and continuous business activities in Singapore is disallowed from enjoying the capital gains exemption.

For the purposes of the capital gains tax exemption, a company is not a shell company if:

- It is listed on recognised stock exchanges of the Contracting State
- Its total annual expenditure on operations in the Residence State is equal to or more than S$200,000 or Indian Rs 50, 00,000 in the respective Contracting State as the case may be, in the immediately preceding period of 24 months from the date the gains arise.

The capital gains tax exemption regime of a country is an important consideration for investors and this exemption, which was

*India-Singapore CECA-Information Kit, Ministry of Trade and Industry, Government of Singapore

previously only available to Mauritius, will help promote greater investment flows between Singapore and India.

Trade In Goods

The Trade in Goods Chapter provides for tariff concessions that will make Singapore goods more competitive vis-à-vis other foreign imports into India. Tariffs on approximately 75% of Singapore's domestic exports will be eliminated or substantially reduced within 5 years. The sectors benefiting includes electrical and electronics, instrumentation, pharmaceuticals, and plastics.

For Singaporean goods entering India, those that qualify for tariff concessions are classified into one of the following categories: immediate elimination, phased elimination and phased reduction. Goods in the immediate elimination category will have tariffs on them eliminated completely when CECA comes into effect. For goods in the phased elimination and phased reduction categories, the reduction to the final tariffs will be phased in over 5 years and the percentage reduction is expressed as a margin of preference over the Most Favored Nation (MFN) applied rates. This is shown in the Table-6 below.

Table 6 : Timeline for the Phased Tariff Concessions

	Tariff reduction by date CECA enters into force (1.8.2005)	*Tariff reduction by 1.4.2006*	*Tariff reduction by 1.4.2007*	*Tariff reduction by 1.4.2008*	*Tariff reduction by 1.4.2009*
Goods qualifying for phased tariff elimination	10%	25%	50%	75%	100%
Goods qualifying for phased tariff reduction	5%	10%	20%	35%	50%

To illustrate phased tariff concessions, we can use an Indian HS tariff line as an example. If the tariff line has an MFN rate of 10% in May 2009, a 50% reduction under Phased Tariff Reduction means that an import duty of 5% would be imposed on the Singapore-originating good entering India.

For Indian goods entering Singapore, Singapore has committed to grant zero-tariff treatment on all imports from India as of entry into force of the Agreement. For example, tariffs on Indian beer entering Singapore will be eliminated.

Rules of Origin

Rules of Origin (ROO) identify the "nationality" of a good. They ensure that only Singaporean or Indian goods enjoy the tariff concessions under CECA.

The general rule of origin is a combination of 40% local content and a change in tariff classification at the 4-digit level. CECA also take into consideration the unique production pattern of Singapore and provides for a list of products that are exempt from the general rule. For each of these products, a specific rule of origin (eg, change in tariff classification only) has been crafted.

Customs

Good customs procedures are necessary to ensure the free movement of goods traded between both countries. The lack of such procedures can increase compliance costs and diminish the benefits that result from tariff reduction.

Under CECA, the customs authorities from India and Singapore will:

- Provide an advance ruling on the eligibility of originating goods for preferential tariffs and tariff classification, upon the request of the trader. This will provide traders with greater certainty on the status of their goods at the country of import.
- Enhance the application of risk management to focus on high-risk goods and facilitate the clearance of low risk consignments. Both authorities will also enhance transparency in regulations so that traders would be fully aware of the requirements and procedures in the respective countries.

Standards and Technical Regulations, Sanitary and Phytosanitary Measures

CECA provides a framework for concluding Mutual Recognition Agreements (MRAs) to eliminate duplicative testing and certification of products to facilitate entry of goods for sale in the respective markets. These sectoral MRAs serve to reduce costs and shorten time to market especially useful for products with short life cycle.

Two sectoral annexes for trade in electrical and electronic products, and telecommunication equipment were concluded under the framework chapter. For products in these two sectors, testing and certification to Indian standards and technical regulations can be done at source. They do not have to be further tested or re-certified on arrival in the market.

The potential benefits are reduction in cost due to elimination of duplicative testing and reduction in time to market for these products to enter the Indian or Singapore market. As most of these products have relatively short life cycles, the result is a reduction in relative cost and improved time to-market competitiveness of Singapore certified products entering the Indian market and vice versa. India is expected to make the necessary amendments to its legislation to implement these MRA arrangements. This may take another 12 – 18 months. Singapore will also be providing technical training for Indian standards bodies so as to enable them to implement the MRA.

Of immediate benefit is the food sectoral annex where Singapore has facilitated the import of egg products, dairy products and packaged drinking water from India. This will widen the sources of supply for these food products in Singapore.

Investment

The investment chapter aims to promote and protect investments from both countries. Market access for investments is based on the principle of National Treatment subject to the commitments or reservations undertaken. The chapter contains a number of useful features to protect investments. The key features are highlighted as follows:—

- Beneficiaries: Citizens and Enterprises based in Singapore or India. Indian investors are not required to seek foreign investment approval for coverage under the investment chapter.

- Broad Range of Investment Instruments: The chapter covers a broad range of investment instruments and assets, such as equity and debt instruments, Intellectual Property Rights (IPR) and, business licenses and permits. Investments in the nature of both Foreign Direct Investment (FDI) and portfolio investments are covered.

- National Treatment: The chapter accords National Treatment to investors from both countries. The market access feature of this provision is subject to the commitments and reservations undertaken.

- Expropriation and Compensation: Both countries cannot expropriate investments, directly or indirectly, without proper legal safeguards. Expropriation must be premised on public purpose and compensation based on market value. Land expropriation will be governed by the domestic legislation of each country.

- Investor to State dispute settlement: To give investors greater confidence in investing in either country, both countries have committed to allowing investors, once the investment is established, to take a dispute relating to an obligation under the chapter to an international arbitration tribunal.

- Free Transfers: Both countries will allow the investors to freely transfer funds related to their investments, such as capital, profits, dividends and royalties.

- Joint-Ventures: India has agreed to bind its recent liberalization measures regulating the ability of current joint-ventures to enter into new joint-ventures (India's Press Note 1 of 2005).

- Real Estate: India has agreed to bind its new regulations governing investments in the real estate sector (India's Press Note 2 of 2005).

Others: The Indian government has formally recognised Temasek and GIC as distinct entities. They are allowed to each own up to 10% of a listed Indian company, similar to other Foreign Institutional Investors (FII), as stipulated under current Securities and Exchange Board of India (SEBI) regulations.

Trade in Services

The services chapter ensures that service suppliers in India and Singapore are guaranteed access into each other's markets. The key features are highlighted as follows:

- Market Access: Both countries may not restrict access into their services market by imposing quantitative restrictions (e.g. numerical quotas on services suppliers that are allowed in the market).
- National Treatment: Services suppliers will be granted the same treatment as local service suppliers, i.e., no discrimination.
- Domestic Regulation: The chapter ensures that domestic regulations governing the provision of services are reasonable, impartial and objective.
- Mutual Recognition Agreements (MRAs): The chapter facilitates the freer movement of people. Professional bodies in the accounting and auditing, architecture, medical (doctors), dental and nursing services sectors in both countries will negotiate agreements, within a year of the signing of CECA, recognising each other's education and professional qualifications. This means that upon the completion of these mutual recognition agreements, Indian and Singaporean professionals from these five professions could be able to practice in Singapore and India respectively. Professional bodies for services sectors not listed above would also be encouraged to enter into negotiations for MRAs.

The services commitments made by each country can be found in the Annexes to the Services Chapter. There are additional disciplines pertaining to Telecommunication Services and Financial Services in their respective Annexes to the Services Chapter.

Generally, the benefits of the CECA will extend to the citizens, permanent residents, local companies as well as foreign MNCs that are constituted or otherwise organised in India or Singapore. Companies wishing to supply audio-visual, educational, financial and telecommunication services, through commercial presence in India or Singapore, would have to meet ownership or control criteria in order to benefit from the CECA.

Both countries have committed to liberalise various services sectors beyond its WTO commitments.

The sectors which Singapore gets preferential access include business services, construction and related engineering services, financial services, telecommunication services, tourism and travel related services and transport services.

India would be able to enjoy preferential treatment for sectors such as business services, distribution services, education services, environmental services and transportation services.

- For Financial Services, Singapore owned or controlled financial institutions have been given greater privileges to access the Indian market. In banking, DBS, UOB and OCBC can each set up a wholly owned subsidiary (WOS) in India to enjoy treatment on par with Indian banks in branching, places of operations and prudential requirements. Alternatively, should they choose to set up as branches, they have been allocated a separate quota of 15 branches (for all 3 banks) over 4 years, over and above the quota for all foreign banks.
- For asset management, Singapore owned or controlled fund managers have the additional privilege of offering Indian investors mutual funds and collective investment schemes (CIS) listed on the Singapore Exchange (SGX) as well as exchange traded funds (ETF). These instruments offered by our asset managers are free from the restriction that they must only invest in entities which have a stake in Indian

companies. India has similarly lifted this limitation for India owned or controlled fund managers. Both Singapore and India owned or controlled fund managers can also invest an additional US$250m in equities and instruments listed on the SGX, including mutual funds, CIS and ETFs. This is in addition to the US$1 billion cap that all asset managers can invest abroad.

- Indian banks and financial institutions can take advantage of CECA to expand their activities in Singapore. To this end, Indian banks, that satisfy Singapore's admission criteria, will be given Wholesale Bank licences and up to 3 bank licences with Qualifying Full Banks privileges. In addition, India insurers and capital market intermediaries that satisfy our admission criteria will have open access to set up in Singapore.
- For Telecommunication Services, India will bind its foreign equity limit from 25% to 49% for most services including basic, cellular and long-distance services and 74% for internet and infrastructure services. India will also ensure that telecommunication providers from Singapore are treated fairly, transparently, and allowed to obtain access to the necessary public infrastructure in order to offer their services, thereby creating a more level playing field in India for our Singapore's telecom providers. On its part, Singapore has made binding commitments for telecommunication services such as Basic Telecommunication Services (facilities-based), Mobile Services, and Value-Added Network (VAN) Services.

Air Services

India and Singapore have reaffirmed their rights and obligations under previous agreements and recognise the importance of air connectivity to support the expansion of tourism, trade and investments.

Both countries will review and enhance further air services linkages through the bilateral Air Services Agreement, in future.

Movement of Natural Persons

The cross-border movement of natural persons plays a central role in initiating and supporting trade and investments in goods and services. This chapter enhances trade and investment flows by facilitating easier temporary entry for 4 categories of business persons from India and Singapore:

- Business Visitors who are holders of five year multiple journey visa will be permitted to enter and engage in business activities for a period of up to 2 months, which upon request, may be further extended by up to 1 month.
- Short-term service suppliers will be granted temporary entry to service their contracts for an initial period of up to 90 days in the first instance.
- Professionals employed in 127 specific occupations will be allowed entry and stay for up to 1 year or the duration of contract, whichever is less.
- Intra-corporate transferees (i.e. managers, executives and specialists within organisations) will be permitted to stay and work in India and Singapore for an initial period of up to 2 years or the period of the contract, whichever is less. The period of stay may be extended for period of up to 3 years at a time for a total term not exceeding 8 years.

The Movement of Natural Persons chapter does not apply to measures regarding citizenship, residence or employment on a permanent basis. It also does not apply to immigration measures as long as these immigration measures do not nullify or impair the commitments made by either country.

The chapter will grant Singaporean and Indian Citizens and Permanent Residents guaranteed entry and stay in each other's country as business visitors, short-term service suppliers, professionals and intra-corporate transferees.

Singapore companies will have certainty when they choose to deploy Singapore staff to help manage their Indian operations. Skilled and qualified professionals and service suppliers from Singapore would also gain easier access to the vast Indian market. Similarly, this would also apply to Indian companies when they deploy Indian staff to manage their operations in Singapore.

With freer movement of business persons between countries, bilateral trade and investment flows should be significantly enhanced. Hence, companies from both countries can leverage on the chapter to drive greater economic integration between India and Singapore.

E-commerce

Both India and Singapore reaffirm their commitment to promote a liberalised environment for electronic commerce. The chapter on electronic commerce addresses fair treatment of digital products, such as software, e-books and e-movies, coming from Singapore.

The Agreement also prohibits any imposition of customs duties on digital products delivered electronically. In addition, both sides commit to ensuring transparency by making publicly available all relevant laws and regulations affecting electronic commerce.

Intellectual Property

The Chapter on Intellectual Property (IP) Cooperation is focused on collaboration and cooperation between the Parties.

The Parties agreed to undertake and promote mutually beneficial cooperation in the fields of IP and Plant Variety Rights. These forms of cooperation could include the joint organisation of training programs, and collaboration on projects to promote the effective use and application of IP. The Parties have specifically identified their leading training centres: the IP Academy, Singapore, and the Intellectual Property Training Institute (Nagpur), as initial partners for cooperation.

The provisions on cooperation and collaboration in IP and training arrived at under the Chapter paves the way forward for collaboration between the Parties in the development of key IP programmes and IP infrastructure. Singapore and India benefit mutually in terms of potential exchange on IP and IP-related training and education programmes. In addition, the mutual recognition of the importance of plant variety rights means that both Singapore and India will be able to consider cooperation activities in this field.

Science & Technology

The Science and Technology cooperation chapter will allow for the fostering of closer collaboration in research and development and commercialisation of technologies between the scientific and research communities from the two countries. It expands an earlier agreement on science and technology signed in 1995.

The agreement is geared towards harnessing the complementary capabilities available in the two countries. The areas of focus that have been identified for possible cooperation are marine and agricultural biotechnology, space research, advance materials and information technology.

Education

The education cooperation chapter is aimed at combining the strengths of the education system in India and Singapore to the mutual benefit of the two countries.

One of its key mandates is to facilitate joint post-graduate programs between the world-renowned Indian Institutes of Technology (IIT) and Institute of Science (IISc) with the Singapore universities. These programs will focus on research and education with clear industrial linkages to companies from both countries. Arising from this, NUS and IIT Bombay have recently signed an MOU to establish a joint graduate engineering programme. The NUS-IIT-B tie-up is the first alliance by any IIT with a foreign university in a significant manner. The programme will draw heavily on existing NUS and IIT-B infrastructure and course modules. Both IIT-B and NUS professors will participate in joint teaching and supervision of projects. The partnership is expected to yield some 40 MS and eight PhD graduates annually.

The chapter also provides that degrees specified by the University Grants Commission of India or an Institution of National

Importance of India, and by universities in Singapore, shall be recognised for the purposes of admission into the universities of both countries. This is in addition to all other admission criteria that must still be satisfied.

A Joint Committee on Education will be established to emphasise the key role that education will play in fostering the relationship between the two countries. Its members will be drawn not only from government but from the private sector as well.

Media

The media cooperation chapter offers a platform for the regulatory agencies from both sides to work closely together. This will allow focus not only on regulatory issues of mutual concern, but more importantly on promoting greater industry and private sector collaboration. Some of the areas of collaboration that could be looked into are digital media and convergent services, intellectual property rights, education and training, co production of film and television content, distribution and marketing, and research and development.

Dispute Settlement

In any international agreement, whilst we do not expect nor hope for disputes between the Parties as to what the agreement means, it would nevertheless be prudent to prepare for such an eventuality. In this connection, Singapore and India have negotiated a comprehensive set of dispute settlement procedures. Disputes are subject to consultations, negotiations, conciliation and arbitration just like in the WTO, thereby enhancing the rule of law in international trade.

Review

The Ministers of India and Singapore, who are responsible for trade negotiations, will meet within a year of the date of entry into force of CECA for a review. Subsequent reviews will be done biennially or otherwise as appropriate.

Conclusions

The intermeshing of Indian and Singaporean areas of concern in trade augurs well for both countries.Singapore is looking out for viable and lucrative destinations besides China and the US, and India is well placed both economically and diplomatically to forge an effective and mutually beneficial partnership.

Thus the increasing diplomatic complementarities and synergies of the two countries in trade and investment, will act as a stabilizing force in the Asia-Pacific region.

REFERENCES

1. *India-Singapore CECA-Information Kit*, Ministry of Trade and Industry, Government of Singapore, 2005.
2. *US Country Commercial Guides*-Singapore, 2004.
3. *Singapore Economic Development Board*-Reports, 2003-2005.
4. *Country Studies-Singapore*, 2005, Microsoft Internet Explorer
5. Rajesh Mehta, *Economic Cooperation between India and Singapore: A Feasibility Study*, RIS-DP # 41/2003.
6. Margaret Liang, *Singapore's Trade Policies-Priorities and Options*, ASEAN Economic Bulletin, Vol.22, No.1 (2005).
7. *Trade Policy Review*: Singapore, WTO, Geneva, 2004.
8. Goh Chok Tong, *Anchored in Singapore, Connected to the World*, Speech at the International Enterprise Forum, Singapore, February 2005.
9. *Foreign Equity Investments in Singapore,* Department of Statistics, Singapore 2001-2002.
10. *Yearbook of Statistics,* Department of Statistics, Singapore 2004.
11. Gaur, S, *ASEAN-India Ties Entering a New Phase*, Business Times, Singapore, 2004.
12. Kumar,N,*Towards an Asian Economic Community: The Relevance of India,* RIS-DP #34/2002
13. Sarma,A and P.K Mehta, *Exploring Indo-ASEAN Economic Partnership in a Globalising World ,Bookwell*, New Delhi, 2002.

14. Rahul Sen, M.G Asher, and R.S Rajan, *ASEAN-India Economic Relations-Current Status and Future Prospects,* Economic and Political Weekly, 2004.

15. Lee Hsien Loong, Speech delivered at the CII, FICCI, ASSOCHEM, Joint Forum, New Delhi, 2005.

16. Bharat Jhunjhunwala, *Singapore FTA: Against Asian Unity?* Business Line, New Delhi, 2005.

17. Frederic Gare and Mattoo, A, *India and ASEAN: The Politics of India's Look East Policy,* Manohar Publishers, New Delhi, 2001.

18. Jha, P.K, *Reassessing India's Look East Policy*, World Focus, Vol. 287-288, 2003.

19. Saywell, T, *Singapore's New India Play*, Far Eastern Economic Review,Singapore, 2001.

16

INDIA AND THE EUROPEAN UNION-MULTI-CULTURALISM AND CONTESTED IDENTITIES

India and the European Union (EU) are the two largest democracies in the world, sharing a common bond of pluralism, consultation, consensus, and rule of law, strength of democratic institutions, a strong and free press, and an independent judiciary. These are the principal features defining their strategic partnership. These principles help manage their continental-sized polities and economies. Decision-making structures are federative, inclusive, caring and conciliatory.

India and the EU are the foremost examples of multiculturalism, that countries elsewhere in the world must embrace as an inevitable consequence of globalization, and the new world order. India views the EU as an independent and indispensable pillar of a world edifice resting on multiple pillars, capable of making significant contributions towards fostering a rule-based international order, and in coming to terms with the challenges of managing global interdependence. The EU is India's largest trading partner, and source of foreign direct investment (FDI). Our economic partnership is based on firm foundations. Indian companies are investing in sectors as diverse as IT (information technology), bio-technology, food-processing, automotive components, and pharmaceuticals.

India sees the EU as a natural partner in its economic development, and interaction with the rest of the world. The strategic partnership is no longer economic-driven, but covers diverse areas of engagement. We share a mutuality of interests on many global issues. We are partners in an intensified fight against terrorism, nuclear proliferation, unsustainable-environment, and sectarian conflict. When the EU-the world's biggest trading bloc and the largest integrated single market economy co-operates with India- the second most populous nation and the fourth largest, fast growing economy, the significance of the partnership goes beyond bilateral relations and impacts on global equations.

The EU sees Indian multiculturalism and its apparent success, as an example where one can learn from each other's experience. In EU circles it is felt if India can exist as a mosaic of ethnicities, religions, languages and cultures, why can't Europe follow the same path?

At the superficial level, there are plenty of similarities between the EU and India. The EU comprises 25 nations with more queuing up. India has 28 states, each marked by a distinctive culture, and 18 official languages. Christianity is the primary religion in Europe: Hinduism in India. Both EU and India have significant minority populations. But, ofcourse, there are profound differences too. Europe after all is the cradle of modern nationalism, and some members of the EU are the oldest nation-states in the world. Thus, howevermuch the EU tries to gloss over angularities of nationalism, it continues to stumble on them.

What the claim to equate EU with India does is to posit civilizational basis for Europe. The problem with this formulation came to the fore when both France and the Netherlands rejected the European constitution. An important reason for this is strong nationalist sentiments in both countries, as opposed to pan-European identities. The attitude to a particular religious minority-Muslims- in Europe bring to the fore EU's policy of multicultural harmonization. As a greater number of Muslims, many of them belonging to a generation raised and nurtured in Europe, are implicated in terrorist acts, EU member-states" policies towards minorities and migration is being severely tested.

17

INDIA AND SOUTH-EAST ASIA : CIVILIZATIONAL TIES AND NEW PARTNERSHIPS

Background

ASEAN or the Association of South East Asian Nations is a political, economic and cultural organization of countries of South East Asia. The original signatories of ASEAN Declaration at Bangkok, signed in 1967 were Indonesia, Malaysia, the Philippines, Singapore and Thailand. The Sultanate of Brunei became a member in 1984. In mid-1995, Vietnam gained admission as the seventh member of ASEAN. Laos and Myanmar followed suit two years later in 1997, and Cambodia joined in 1999. Thus, ASEAN today has 10 members, covering all the countries of South East Asia from Myanmar in the extreme West to Vietnam in the extreme East.

Asian developing countries have made a number of attempts at regional cooperation in the 1970s with UN ESCAP's (Economic and Social Commission of Asia and Pacific) initiative. These include the Bangkok Agreement established in 1975, which covered exchange of tariff concessions between five member governments, viz. Bangladesh, India, Laos, South Korea and Sri Lanka. The Asian Clearing Union (ACU) with seven members in the region viz. Bangladesh, India, Iran, Myanmar, Nepal, Pakistan, and Sri Lanka came into being in 1974. These early experiences have not been very successful. The Bangkok Agreement suffered from limited coverage of membership and preference margins were not deep enough, and scope not extending to non-tariff barriers.

Territorial Ambit of Asia

Asia is essentially a geographical expression. It covers the Arabic-speaking countries in West Asia, Israel, Turkey and Iran. South Asia includes Afghanistan (SAARC countries-Afghanistan will become a member of SAARC in 2007). South East Asia includes ASEAN. East Asia groups China, the Korean peninsula and Japan. These countries constitute a variety of ethnic groups, languages and faiths. Historically there has been no evolution of an "Asian entity" or an "Asian identity". This is in marked contrast to the unifying embrace of a Hispanic identity which brings the people of South and Central America together, a Caribbean identity, an African identity, a North American identity and a European identity. This sense of shared identity has already found institutional expression in the European Union, the Organization of American States, or the African Union (AU). In contrast, in Asia there are at least three groupings-the Arabic speaking countries of West Asia, ASEAN and SAARC. The remaining countries remain territorially unaffiliated. The UN (United Nations) however divides Asia between its Arabic-speaking members in the Economic Commission for West Asia and all other Asian countries into ESCAP which brings together the Asian countries with countries of the Pacific as well ranging from Australia and New Zealand to diverse island countries of the Pacific like Togo and Vanuatu. It is only in the last few years of the last century and more so in the present century that one talks of a unified Asian century. The Asian countries will also now include the Asian Republics of the former Soviet Union.

Even today when we talk of an *"Asian Century"*, we only include ASEAN, China, Japan, Korea and India. West Asia, Central Eurasian Countries (former Asian Soviet Republics), other SAARC countries are ignored.

Asia is a region of *"multiple heterogeneities"*—namely geographical, economic, political and social. The region does not lack resources, but lacks initiatives for building complementarities. A closing of the ranks in the whole of Asia will ensure greater reciprocity in economic relations with Europe and North America.

The size and dynamism of the Asian economy is a potentially autonomous engine of growth, which need not exclusively depend on the health and policy compulsions of Europe and North America. The Asian region as whole together accounts, today for 40% of global exports, 30% of global imports, 50% of global international reserves. A dynamic Asian economy could compensate to a substantial degree for sluggish growth elsewhere. This growth potential derives from the large and diversified natural resource base and productive structures in the region. Its member countries produce everything from energy, vital minerals, tropical products, fibres and cereals. It covers industrial and trading capacities ranging from the most capital-intensive to the most labour-intensive, with a large and varied work force commanding different compensation levels. All these factors are highly conducive to a greater economic interaction. Some strategic observers have even noted that it may be desirable to take on even Pakistan on board in a future Asian alliance. Thus we should have an Asian economic and strategic architecture-East Asia Summit, Asian Energy Grid+SCO (Shangai Co-operative Organization).

Regional Cooperation and Integration

Regional cooperation is a more "general" term than integration, where two or more countries come together for mutual benefit-it may take the form of

- Technology transfer
- Shared managerial expertise
- Joint production and marketing facilities, besides
- Pure commodity trade

Economic integration is a "narrower" term. The word integration was first used in the field of "industrial organization", meaning a combination of business firms through agreements, cartels, trusts and mergers. Prof. Jan Tinbergen first used the term in his book "International Economic Integration" (1954) and the term was further refined by giving an analytical account of concepts and strategies of economic integration across nations in Bela Belassa in his Book "Theory of Economic Integration" (1961).

The motivating factors for integration or more particularly, what is defined in the literature as RTAs or Regional Trading Arrangements (RTAs) are–

- Regional cooperation can be effective in exploiting regional complementarities and economies of scale.
- Regional cooperation by bringing about diplomatic cohesion, can reduce regional tensions, and can be effective in keeping out negative extra-regional influences.
- Regional cooperation can lead to industrial restructuring and more efficient production structures within individual countries-that is efficiency-induced domestic industrial restructuring.
- Smaller countries can get increased "security of market access" and "safe havens" by forming RTAs.
- Unilateral domestic policy reforms can be locked-in, once RTAs are formed.
- Countries in RTAs can improve their bargaining power in MTNs (Multilateral Trade Negotiations).
- Industries can be promoted that are not viable without protected regional markets-regional infant industries-the idea being that they would be internationally competitive if given sufficient time to develop.
- RTAs can offer quicker solution for freer word trade, than "multilateralism", which is slower.
- Article 24 of WTO, says that RTAs are consistent with globalization.
- Intra-regional trade liberalization increases competition for industries of the region, improves technical and business complementarity and also attracts FDI.

The major regional organizations in Asia (besides ASEAN) are—

1. GCC (Gulf Cooperation Council) established in 1981-it has six Arab states-Bahrain, Kuwait, Oman, Qatar, Saudi Arabia and UAE.
2. SAARC (Bangladesh, Bhutan, India, Maldives, Nepal, Pakistan, Sri Lanka) established in 1985. China, Japan will be Observers and Afghanistan a full member in 2007.
3. IOR-ARC (Indian Ocean Rim Association for Regional Cooperation) established in 1997. 19 countries are members. The key players are Australia, India and South Africa.
4. SCO (Shangai Cooperative Organization). China, Russia and five central Asian Republics-Kyrgyzsthan, Kazakhstan, Turkmenistan, Tadjikstan and Uzbekistan are members. Pakistan, Iran and, India are observers.
5. APEC (Asia Pacific Economic Cooperation forum) formed in 1993. It is based on "Open Regionalism". Voluntary action and consensual decisions form the basis of cooperation.
6. It is a regional non-starter, too diverse, geographically scattered, and no meaningful integration. The areas of voluntary action are-
   - Trade liberalization
   - Trade facilitation
   - Investment facilitation
   - Sectoral cooperation projects also play an important role.

Today, over 60% of world trade is routed through RTAs or PTAs, and around 40% through multilateral or MFN (Most Favoured Nation) process. Today there are 193 RTAs in the world.

Stages in Integration

There are various stages in the integration process, and levels of cooperation and integration among the participating countries. These are—

1. **PTAs or Preferential Trading Arrangements:** Quantitative restrictions and tariffs between participating countries are reduced, not abolished.

2. **FTAs or Free Trade Areas:** Quantitative restrictions and tariffs between countries are ABOLISHED, but each participant country retains its own tariffs against non-members.

3. **Customs Union:** Participating countries impose the same tariffs on non-members, i. e CET (Common External Tariff).

4. **Common Market:** Restrictions on factor movements are abolished, i. e services and labour movement within the integration area flow freely.

5. **Economic Union:** Monetary policies are harmonized like a common currency in the EU (European Union). Economic and social policies are to some extent harmonized.

6. **Supra National Union:** Governments of participating countries relinquish their sovereignty even over defence and foreign policies to a supra national authority. This has happened to some extent as in the European Parliament, but as the Iraq war has demonstrated there are deep divisions even in Europe over Defence and Foreign Policy objectives.

Details of ASEAN

The Secretariat of ASEAN is located in Jakarta, Indonesia. The official language is English.

Objectives of Asean

1. Economic, social and cultural development of the sub-region.

2. Promotion of peace and stability in the sub-region.

3. Encouragement of cooperation and mutual assistance in areas of common interest.

4. Cooperation in economic, social, cultural, technical, scientific, and administrative fields.

5. Mutual aid in education, professional and vocational training and administration through the provision of training and research facilities.

6. Cooperation to develop agriculture and industry; to expand trade; to develop transport and communication; and to raise the standard of living of inhabitants of the sub-region.

7. Co-operation with international, regional and extra-regional organizations.

Structure

The organizational structure of ASEAN includes-

1. Meeting of ASEAN Heads of State and Government
2. ASEAN Ministerial Conferences
3. Senior Economic Officials Meetings (EOM)
4. ASEAN Secretary General and the ASEAN Secretariat

After the ASEAN annual summit, there is a Post Ministerial Conference (PMC) with its dialogue partners, and an ASEAN Regional Forum (ARF) of 23 members that seeks to address security issues in the Asia-Pacific region. ARF met for the first time in 1994. ASEAN has a +3 dialogue with China, Japan and South Korea and an independent summit with India since 2001.

ASEAN had limited cooperation in economic issues until 1992, when it was decided to set up the AFTA(ASEAN Free Trade Area). AFTA is to be established by 2008.

The main mechanism for implementation of AFTA is the CEPT (Common Effective Preferential Tariff). CEPT tariffs were to be reduced between 0% to 5% by 2003 for the ASEAN-6. The deadline for Vietnam is 2006, and for Myanmar and Laos 2008. AFTA has been complemented with other initiatives to facilitate movement of capital between ASEAN countries. These are principally the AICO (ASEAN Industrial Cooperation Organization) and AIA (ASEAN Investment Area). There has been a marked increase in intra-ASEAN trade. Total intra-ASEAN trade increased from 18% in 1992 to 30% in 2005.

ASEAN has also emerged as a major force in international relations, with the ARF (ASEAN Regional Forum) given great importance by all great powers including China, the U. S, Russia and Japan. The recently concluded high-profile EAS (East Asia Summit) also drew world-wide attention.

India-Asean Linkages

India has moved purposefully in developing a broad economic and strategic partnership with the dynamic countries of South East Asia.

CHRONOLOGY

1991—India's engagement with ASEAN started with its "Look East Policy"

1992—India became a Sectoral Dialogue Partner of ASEAN-Cooperating in Trade, Investment and Tourism.

1996 India became a Full Dialogue Partner and an active participant in the ARF. ARF met for the first time in 1994.

2001 ASEAN-INDIA relationship upgraded to the summit level.

2002 First ASEAN-INDIA Summit in Phnom Penh

2003 Second ASEAN-INDIA Summit in Bali concluded with the signing of three major documents-

- Framework Agreement for Comprehensive Economic Cooperation.
- Accession Document to the TAC (Treaty of Amity and Co-operation)
- Adoption of the Joint Declaration on Cooperation in Combating International Terrorism

2004 Third ASEAN-India Summit in Vientiane, capital of Laos. Agreement on "India-ASEAN Partnership for Peace, Progress, and Shared Prosperity".

2005 Fourth ASEAN-INDIA Summit in Kuala Lumpur, Malaysia. India's high profile role established in the East Asia Summit, with ASEAN, Japan, Korea, China, Australia and New Zealand. (16 countries). India-ASEAN Free Trade Area (FTA) to come into force in 2007.

India has an FTA with Thailand and a A (Comprehensive Economic Cooperation Agreement was signed with Singapore in 2005.

There are two other sub-regional partnerships which India has in the ASEAN region. These are—

- MGC (Mekong-Ganga Cooperative Forum) floated by India with 5 of its Eastern neighbours-Myanmar, Thailand, Cambodia, Vietnam and Laos in 2001. Tourism, culture and education are given precedence and priority in the cooperative framework. Transport, Communication, and Infrastructure are next areas of priority.
- BIMSTEC (Bay of Bengal Initiative for Multi-Sectoral Technical and Economic Cooperation). The first summit was held in Bangkok in July 2004. Part of India's immediate and intermediate neighbourhood policy and includes-1. India 2. Bangladesh 3. Bhutan 4. Myanmar 5. Thailand 6. Nepal 7. Cambodia 8. Vietnam and 9. Laos.

The Mekong basin has the potential to emerge as a major granary as its vast lands are very fertile. India and Thailand can do much to tame the Mekong River, and enhance cultivation by spreading irrigation.

An unfortunate fact of history is that despite strong civilizational ties with South East Asia dating back to centuries, and despite the Indian diaspora scattered around many countries of the ASEAN region, India failed in its efforts to befriend the countries of the region in the recent past.

India's first contacts with Southeast Asia began in the Maurayan dynasty, when emissaries of Ashoka spread Buddhism across the region. In the first century AD, the migration of Indian princes, priests, poets and artisans triggered off cultural efflorescence in South East Asian countries. The greatest temples of Vishnu are located not in India, but in South East Asia-like the Angkor Vat- Siam Rep complex in Cambodia, and the biggest Buddha stupa in Boru Budur in Indonesia.

The second phase began with the growth of maritime trade with South East Asia. The Gujarati Muslim merchants, mainly subscribing to the Sufi variant of Islam, played an important role in the Islamisation of Malay peninsula and the Indonesian archipelago. It is primarily for this reason that Islam in South East Asia is more accommodative and "malleable" than the exclusionary Wahibi type of Islam of West Asia. The great sea-faring kings of the 12th century in India established the Khmer and SriVijaya empires. In the colonial times, the vast reservoir of Indian manpower was exploited to serve the colonial interests of Britain. The rubber plantations in Malaya, the backbone of the Malayan economy, and the sugar plantations in the far-flung areas of the British Empire were developed as a result of the exploitation of Indian workers. Today there are 4. 5 million people of Indian origin in South East Asia. They constitute 8% of the population of Malaysia and 7% of the population of Singapore.

Some useful facts highlighting the close civilizational contacts between India and Malaysia are instructive—

- The Ramayana in its variations is the national epic of both Indonesia and Thailand.
- The King of Thailand, a Buddhist country, traces his origin to Rama, and is considered the 9th incarnate of Rama.
- The symbol "Ganesha" is embossed on the Indonesian Rupaiah.
- Many words of Indian/Sanskrit origin are found in South East Asia. Singapore comes from "Singhapura" or Lion City. Brunei comes from the word Braun or "Varun", the Hindu God. The PM of Malaysia is called "Prathan Mantri", as are many other words in "Basha Malaya".
- Modern day Orissa still commemorates, the great Kalinga kings conquests in modern-day Indonesia by a festival called Bali Jatra, where tiny boats with lamps on them are allowed to sail from the coast of Orissa.

- In modern times, the President of Singapore, Mr. Nathan is of Indian (Tamil origin), as are Cabinet ministers of Malaysia. The name of a former Indonesian President "Megawati" Sukarnoputri was given by the Orissa leader Biju Patnaik.

ASEAN and India are today geographically contiguous, as Myanmar shares a long border with the North East States of India. The Southernmost tip of Andaman and Nicobar Islands, Indira Point, is just 40 KM from Aceh in Indonesia. The effect of this was adequately demonstrated in the Tsunami, when the Andaman's were more seriously affected than even other parts of Indonesia.

Independent India's engagement with ASIA began under Jawaharlal Nehru. Under Nehru's leadership, the Asian Relation's Conference was organized in 1947, and the special conference on Indonesia in 1949. India also played an important role in organizing the Bandung Conference on Afro-Asian solidarity in 1955. Such was India's stature, that India was given Chairmanship of the International Control Commission of Vietnam, Laos and Cambodia in 1954, as per the Geneva Agreement, which was supposed to unify North and South Vietnam after the French left Indo-China.

However, India gradually began to get disillusioned with Asia, as the U. S began to isolate India with regional pacts like CENTO and SEATO. The Chinese also began to get overassertive, and India's complete disillusionment of playing a greater role in Asia, came with the Sino-Indian war of 1962. The Pakistan aggression of 1965, also made India turn away from her immediate neighbourhood. India at the same time began forging close ties both politically and economically with the Soviet Union. It must be admitted that the Soviet Union played a stellar role in shaping India's infrastructure, by helping India build her steel plants and large irrigation dams (which Nehru called the "Temples of Modern India"), the benefits of which India is reaping even today. Also, the Soviet Union helped India politically and in the defence sphere, and was a timely ally in India's moments of crisis. The Defence relationship continues even today, with more than 70% of our defence equipment still coming from Russia, although India has a strategic relationship with the United States, after the Indo-US Nuclear Agreement.

India's geo-political and more so geo-economic compulsions of allying with the FSU (Former Soviet Union), and away from Asia in the 1960s and 1970s must thus be viewed in its totality. Such was Nehru's disillusionment with Asia, that when Tunku Abdul Rahman, the former Prime Minister of Malaysia, and Lee Kuan Yew, the former Prime Minister of Singapore, approached him with the idea of forming an economic alliance with South East Asia, he tersely told them—"I have nothing to do with the Cocoa Cola economies". Prime Minister Indira Gandhi, also assiduously forged ties with the Indo-Chinese States, particularly Vietnam in the cold-war days. Support for India's association with the expanded ASEAN region is readily forthcoming because of Indira Gandhi's initiatives in the 1970s and 1980s. Rajiv Gandhi also played a role in renewing ties with Asia, with his path-breaking visit to China in 1988. His hand-shake with the legendary Chinese leader Deng Xiao Ping, set of a chain-reaction in restructuring Sino-Indian and India-Asia relations.

India initially perceived the establishment of ASEAN as an extension of the American sphere of influence. It viewed the origin of ASEAN as being political in its nature using regional economic co-operation merely as a rational for justifying its existence. The ASEAN countries viewed India as a satellite of the former Soviet Union. India's pro-Soviet line of handling its foreign policy on Vietnam and Cambodia in the 1970s and 1980s irked most of the ASEAN countries, and added to the political distance between India and ASEAN

India's relatively closed economy before 1990 also did not provoke interest among ASEAN, which had changed their strategies since the early 1970s towards outward-looking and more open economies. Lee Kuan Yew even advised Indira Gandhi "you may be non-aligned, but align yourself with the international market grid, and gate crash into the free market"

With the collapse of the Berlin Wall in 1989, and the disintegration of the Soviet Union soon after, the political freeze in relations between India and ASEAN made no sense. The improvement of India's relations with China since the mid-1980s, also improved the political environment in the ASEAN countries for strengthening economic co-operation with India. India's post-1991 economic reforms transformed the Indian economy to an attractive destination for expanding and diversifying the market for ASEAN exports. This has been very nicely put by Thomas Friedman in his book, "The World is Flat", in the chapter "When the Walls Came Down, and the Windows Went Up".

The ASEAN countries also discovered several new complementarities among their economies, and the Indian economy. The surplus capital of some of the ASEAN countries could be put to good economic use by combining it with the globally recognized skills of scientific, technical, professional, and managerial manpower of India. India's defence capabilities, non-aggressive historical record and commitment to maintenance of peace in the world and in Asia are recognized.

The combined effect of the fundamentally altered economic, political and strategic environment in the ASEAN region, led the ASEAN grouping to clearly recognize the mutual benefits of strengthening economic relations with India.

The foundations of India's "Look East" policy were laid by Prime Minister P. V Narasimha Rao. His famous Singapore lecture of 1994 in which he announced India's intention to use the Asia-Pacific region "as a spring board for India's leap into the global market-place" ushered in India's new engagement with Asia. The "Look East" initiatives are now pursued with renewed vigour, and today what we need is a "Focus East" policy. Today, India's "Gaze" towards ASEAN is so strong, that China and the United States are beginning to get wary of us.

The next step for India is to look beyond the ASEAN-East Asian region, and extend the policy to the vast Asia-Pacific region. It should also cover besides economic, strategic and socio-cultural issues as well. There is much scope for further expanding and deepening our co-operative agenda, synergizing the economies of India and the ASEAN and exploring new avenues for diplomatic complementarities.

India-ASEAN co-operation has progressed substantially in many spheres-mainly in science and technology, tourism, trade and investment. India's trade with ASEAN currently stands at $18 billion, registering a 35% growth since the 1990s. ASEAN's share in India's global trade is 8. 5%, and was the fastest-growing region for India.

The level of investment flows on both sides also has progressed substantially, but still has a lot of untapped potential.

The relevance of geo-economic relations as the dominant force in shaping the future of international and regional relations is most likely to grow substantially in the 21st century-notwithstanding the expanding role of WTO. In this noticeably altered global and regional context, economic diplomacy will increasingly overshadow the traditional political and geo-strategic dimensions of the foreign policy formulations of the decades to come. A coalitional approach to the management of power relations at the regional levels is most likely to be preferred in the economic sphere. The future battles arising from conflicts of national interests are most likely to be fought in the global. regional markets, rather than on battlefields.

While small-scale or domestic conflicts are undermining peace and security of almost every sub-region in the Indian Ocean, large-scale regional security and strategic matters are also gaining in primacy, including the rise of terrorism. The large foreign military presence, the proliferation of weapons of mass destruction and missile capabilities, the security of sea lanes of communications (SLOCs), as well as smuggling and piracy at sea are getting increasing attention. In the pacific resolution of domestic conflicts, negotiation takes place in specific case by case forums, rather than in large multilateral region-wide

Organisations. Some Indian oceanic multilateral commitments on peace and security issues could certainly help to limit conflict escalation and their negative impact at the sub-regional scale.

Within its three specific protocols, and its regional forum, the ASEAN Regional Forum (ARF) addressing peace, security and stability issues, ASEAN has developed an original framework that could certainly serve as a model for the development of a formal Indian oceanic co-operation on these matters.

It is thus obvious that regional co-operation in peace, security, and strategic matters could help limit ongoing conflict situations, prevent new conflicts, promote disarmament and non-proliferation, and address the role of foreign militaries in the region, thus generating a more stable geo-political environment.

India has recently consciously attempted to provide explicit economic orientation to its foreign policy. India has adopted a sustained "Look East" policy for consciously expanding its economic linkages with ASEAN countries.

India's key position at the head of the Indian Ocean, astride the East-West trade route is n asset. Today, India's strategic influence stretches to both the entry points to the Indian Ocean –from the Straits to the Indian Ocean-from the Straits of Hormuz in the West, to the Straits of Mallaca in the East.

The bulk of India's foreign trade is seaborne; besides protecting its long coast line and SLOCs, it has to adequately patrol her 200km EEZ (Exclusive Economic Zone), where there is frequent poaching by modern and fast South East Asian vessels. Threats from Pakistan and more recently the growing menace of the Chinese Navy, which has started making its presence felt in the Indian Ocean region through the Coco islands in the North Andamans Sea are increasing.

India considers the Indian Ocean region well within its sphere of influence-and thus trade with the South East Asian countries-now all part of the ASEAN-assumes added importance in the emerging geo-economic strategies of India.

Indo-ASEAN co-operation can serve as a stabilising factor in promoting India's geo-strategic interests in the Indian Ocean region.

There is much scope for further expanding and deepening our cooperative agenda, synergising the economies of India and ASEAN and exploring new avenues for diplomatic complementarities.

India-ASEAN cooperation has progressed substantially in many spheres- mainly in science and technology, IT and electronics, HRD, transport and infrastructure, space technology, tourism and trade and investment. These initiatives are however not adequately reflected in trade figures.

India also signed a landmark free-trade agreement with Thailand and four other accords for enhancing co-operation in agriculture, tourism and science. The FTA will provide a free-trade area in goods to begin by 2010, and in services and investment from 2006.

The level of investment flows on both sides has a lot of untapped potential and can easily rise to $ 1 billion by 2007, with sustained efforts by both sides. The redeeming fact is that there are substantial investments by both India and ASEAN in each other's countries.

Although there have been significant changes in commodity composition of India's trade with ASEAN countries in recent years, components of the trade basket could do with substantial revision, with an increasing emphasis on India moving up the value chain.

India should also intensify its marketing thrust to ASEAN countries to correct the asymmetry in trade relations. Both infrastructure and technology can be hawked much more aggresively. Our exporters should negotiate much harder, offer more competitive terms, adhere to delivery schedules, and provide effective after-sales service. A marketing culture among our exporters, combined with a bit of hard sell, could help India make decisive inroads into the ASEAN markets.

Intensive efforts to promote business synergies on the two sides in areas such as infrastructure, IT, biotechnology, and tourism got a positive boost with the India-ASEAN Business Summits. A trade pact with ASEAN is the best beginning since India has traditionally enjoyed many links-economic and strategic- with the region, although there is a lot of untapped potential. However, there are major differences in "tariff rates" between India and the big five of ASEAN. Indian customs duties are on an average at least twice and in many cases thrice as high as in ASEAN. Thus tariff equalization and rationalization will not be easy for a free trade to appear in the near future. Moreover changes to domestic tariff and commercial policy will be difficult because it may hurt the interests of domestic producers.

We should also try to strengthen strategic alliances with the *guanxi (*overseas Chinese networks) who contol most of the distribution channels in Malaysia, Singapore and to some extent Thailand.

India should also make available information on its capabilities in fields like IT, and market these better in countries like the Philippines and Brunei, as trade with these two ASEAN countries is virtually non-existent.

The terms of India-ASEAN engagement needs to be taken much more seriously. The possibilities for functional cooperation are limitless, and enthusiasm should translate into tangible gains. India also needs to deepen her links with MGC (Mekong Ganga Cooperative forum) - a new co-operative forum floated by India with five of its eastern neighbours- Myanmar, Thailand, Cambodia, Vietnam and Laos. Tourism, culture and education are given precedence and priority in the cooperative framework. Transport, communications and infrastructure will be prioritised in the next phase. The MGC also provides immense opportunities for India's private sector to create a niche in the region; India can make up for its past mistakes. Indo-ASEAN cooperation in tourism, culture and education can also be strengthened in Indonesia and Malaysia.

It must be remembered that India's cultural footprints in SouthEast Asia have been left because of trade and religion, and not a show of power.

India's relations with ASEAN assume significance also in the light of the various cultural similarities it shares with the region. Buddhism is the natural link to S-E Asia, particularly the Mekong basin. The cultural ties with S-E Asia need to be stressed apart from trade and Buddhism.

ASEAN can also source its manpower requirements-technical and manegerial- from India, as manpower here is both competitive and culturally compatible. Indian professionals teaching English and computer skills can raise the standards of education and knowledge base. The ASEAN-India HRD programme needs to be further strengthened.

India has today got a new dimension to its Look- east vision- developing its northeastern states by linking them to SouthEast Asia through road and rail links via Myanmar. It is part of a larger project to build Eurasian land and rail corridors that could connect Singapore to Istanbul and Europe via both India and China. The Trans-Continental highway and railway could lead to the ultimate link up of China, Russia and Central Asia, bringing immense benefits to all the countries.

India recently opened the road linking Manipur's Tamu on the border with Myanmar with Kalewa and Kaleymo and from there to Mandalay- the commercial heart of Myanmar.

China has already agreed in principle to build a highway connecting connecting Bangkok with Kunming in the thriving Yunan province of China, through Laos. A road from Kunming to Ruihi on the Chinese border with Myanmar already exists. China is also developing the "Irrawady Corridor" beginning in Kunming and reaching the Western Coast of Myanmar facing the Indian Ocean Rim. China's interior provinces such as Yunnan, Sichuan and Gizhou will no longer have to depend on far away ports on China's eastern sea-board and can have access to the warm waters of the Indian Ocean. Thailand also has plans to build another highway linking it with Vietnam through Laos. That will give Thailand access to the Danang port on the Vietnamese coastilne. To the East, Thailand hopes to connect this road to Moulmein in Myanmar.

There is also a possibility of building a railway line between the Chinese cities of Kunming and Mytikyima on the Myanmar border, where both the roads, Ledo to Patakai Range and Ledo to South Myanmar meet. The Asian Development Bank has given a loan to the Myanmar government to construct the railway through northern Myanmar linking India with China. India thus wants to develop her northeast by using Myanmar as a bridge to economically leverage with China and the other ASEAN nations.

The essence of this triangular road and rail diplomacy among India, China, Myanmar and Thailand is also about ultimately about linking the Indian Ocean to the South China Sea. In economic and strategic terms India wants to develop its north east by increasing its connectivity with the rest of the world through commercial linkages with ASEAN. By taking advantage of Myanmar's links with other ASEAN countries, India hopes to transform the northeast from a *security burden* into a *land of economic opportunity.*

The Mekong basin also has the potential to emerge as a major granary as its vast lands are very fertile. India and Thailand can do much to tame the Mekong River, and enhance cultivation by spreading irrigation.

ASEAN also faces the problem of disparity in development, the new entrants- Laos, Vietnam and Cambodia showing lower levels of performance compared to the other members-and will take time to integrate fully into the ASEAN framework. India can offer its help here as well by providing interest-free credit facilities for speedier development of these countries, and cashing in on the tremendous good-will that existed for her in the cold-war days.

There is also immense scope for further enhancing joint ventures in manufacturing, consultancy, leasing and trading outfits between India and ASEAN.

Other measures to promote greater India-ASEAN interaction should include relaxation of visa restrictions by ASEAN countries much more to facilitate greater collaboration among businessmen and technical personnel, opening up of the financial and banking sector, reduction of non-tariff barriers, sustained improvement in the delivery system of the Indian bureaucracy, and continuing to give explicit economic orientation to foreign policy.

At the geo-political level, India's membership of the ARF (ASEAN Regional Forum), discussing security issues, can serve to effectively protect and project India's strategic interests in the region. While India's membership of ARF enables it to participate in regional security issues, we would seriously undermine our long term strategic and economic interests, if we do not take into account China's rapidly expanding economic and strategic profile in our eastern neighbourhood.

The second phase of India's LookEast policy also coincides with India's *dalliance* with the U. S., as opposed to a formal *alliance.* India today has more intensive security links with America's allies in the

ARF (Asian Regional Forum of ASEAN)-Australia, South Korea and Japan. India's improved ties with the U. S have also created the space for a more confident and constructive engagement with China in both strategic and economic terms. India's "Look East" policy should also be integrated into a larger regionalisation strategy, encompassing South Asia, the Indian Ocean Rim, the Bay of Bengal Rim, and the Asia-Pacific. As SAARC continues to remain moribund because of the ego clashes in the region, and the IOR-ARC faces teething problems and is yet to take off, India's future lies in having a definite focus eastwards-particularly with ASEAN-and strengthening the infrastructural, economic, cultural and commercial relations with these countries.

India's new found enthusiasm to forge a trade pact with ASEAN also stands in stark contrast with its attitude towards SAARC, and even towards bilateral relations with its neighbors in South Asia. That a free trade area in South Asia remains a non-starter is not entirely the fault of Pakistan-India too has been reluctant to make the larger concessions that will make a more effective South Asian grouping.

As India pursues the idea of a free trade zone with ASEAN, it is hoped that simultaneously other regional initiatives lying moribund will also be re-activated, so that the Indian economy develops a multi-layered set of net-works in the larger Asian and Indian Ocean regions.

India-ASEAN Co-operation in Areas other than Politics and Economics

Science and Technology

India's science and technology co-operation with ASEAN has made considerable progress under the dialogue partnership in the mutually identified areas of (a) Advanced Materials, (b) Information Technology, and (c) Bio Technology. India has funded the attachment of eight ASEAN research scientists to Indian research laboratories under the Advanced Materials Project. The "ASEAN-India Digital Archive" project proposes joint collaboration in Information Technology (IT).

Tourism

Tourism is an area where India is keen to link up with ASEAN to promote two-way tourist traffic as well as leverage its complementarities to ASEAN tourist circuits in international tourism markets. Specific Indian destinations for joint marketing with ASEAN are being identified, addressing related tourism infrastructure needs involving investors and taking other promotional and familiarization measures.

ASEAN-India tourism co-operation include—

- Common Marketing Strategy
- Industry Networking
- Image Building
- Networking of Information and Facilitation Services
- Networking of Tourism Training Institutes and Training Programmes on Tourism

Human Resource Development (HRD)

ASEAN and India are jointly committed to conducting expert studies on Indian and ASEAN capabilities and complementarities in this sector. Academic exchange programmes, India Study Centres in ASEAN, ASEAN Study Centres in India, Linking Indian Universities with the ASEAN University Network (AUN), possibility of ASEAN placements in IITs and IIMs.

People-to-People Contacts

An ASEAN-India Eminent Persons Lecture Series was launched with the objective of promoting awareness about the reality and potential of ASEAN-India partnership. This programme is coordinated by RIS (Research and Information System for Non-Aligned Countries), a Government of India sponsored think-thank based in New Delhi. Eminent leaders and opinion makers, senior academics, media personalities, technologists, captains of trade and industry are invited to give public lectures on different aspects of economic, political, cultural and security ties between ASEAN countries and India.

India and South-East Asia-the way Ahead

The East Asia summit (EAS) had sixteen countries attending, - the ASEAN ten, South Korea, Japan, India, China, Australia, and New Zealand. They were all represented by their respective Heads-of-State and Heads-of-Government, at the inaugural summit at Kuala Lumpur, Malaysia. EAS may ultimately evolve into an East Asian Community (EAC) discussing economic and strategic issues. EAC may finally subsume the evolving ASEAN community, to form a larger Asian economic grouping.

No country, particularly China should be allowed to dominate any future visions of an Asian Community, by practicing a "Monroe Doctrine for Asia", seeking absolute influence over the entire East Asian region.

In conclusion, India will need to be strong economically if it has to be recognized as a major regional or global power. Closer economic and political interaction with the economically dynamic group of countries like ASEAN will motivate our decision makers to effect much needed changes in economic institutions and policies to make the economy vibrant and foreign policy more dynamic.

REFERENCES

- Frederic Gare and Amitabh Mattoo (Eds) India and ASEAN-The politics of India's look east policy, *Manohar Publishers*, New Delhi, 2001.
- V. R Panchamukhi and Rehman Sobhan (Eds) Towards an Asian Economic Area, *Macmillan,* New Delhi, 1995.
- Asian economic integration-Vision of a new Asia, *Conference Proceedings, RIS*, Tokyo, November, 2004.
- Sudhir Devare, India and South East Asia-Towards Security Convergence, *ISEAS, Singapore and Capital publishing company,* New Delhi, 2006.
- From deep engagement to strong engagement, *Straits Times*, July, 2005.
- Amitav Acharya, The quest for identity: international relations of South East Asia, *Oxford University Press*, Singapore 2000.

- Roger Cohen, The roar of a new Asia is in the global horizon, *International Herald Tribune*, April, 2005.
- K. S Nathan, (Eds) India and ASEAN: The growing partnership for the twenty-first century, Institute for diplomacy and foreign relations, Kuala Lumpur, 2000.
- Jaswant Singh, Defending India, *McMillan India*, Chennai, 1999.
- Rahul Bedi, A new doctrine for the Indian Navy, *Frontline (India)*, July, 2004.
- Mohammed Ayub, India and South East Asia: Indian perceptions and policies, *Routledge*, New York, 1990.
- Kanti Bajpai, Enhancing Ties between India and South East Asia: An Indian View, in *India South East Asia and the United States: New opportunities and prospects for co-operation edited by Satu P. Limaye and Ahmed Mukarram, , ISEAS, ,* Singapore 1998.
- Ali Alatas, Clash of Civilizations? No it is Pure Evil, *Straits Times*, 16 July, 2004.
- K. S Sulu and A. Macaw, Indian Communities in South East Asia: An Indian View, *ISEAS,* Singapore, 1993.
- Francis Fukuyama, The end of history and the last man, *Free Press,* New York, 1992.

18

INDIA AND THE ASEAN REGIONAL FORUM (ARF)

It is recognised the world over that the current century is an "Asian century" with India, China and ASEAN as the major players in Asia's "economic renaissance." The main challenge of the ARF (ASEAN Regional Forum) is to sustain and enhance peace and prosperity in the East Asian region. ASEAN has undertaken the obligation to be the primary driving force of the ARF. A successful ARF requires the active participation and cooperation of all participants. ASEAN must be sensitive to the interests and concerns of all ARF participants. The "gradualism" of ARF is its strong point, rather than "knee – jerk" reactions or "quick-fix" solutions.

The first ARF was held in Bangkok, Thailand, on 25th July 1994, in accordance with the 1992 Singapore declaration of the fourth ASEAN Summit, where it was proclaimed their intent to intensify ASEAN's external dialogues in political and security, matters as a means of building tries with states in the Asia–Pacific region. It was agreed that as a high–level consultative forum, the ARF had enabled the countries in the Asia–Pacific region to foster the habit of constructive dialogue and consultation on political and security issues of common interest and concern. In this respect, the ARF would be in a position to make significant contributions to efforts towards confidence building and preventive in the wider Asia–Pacific region.

It must be realised ARF is not a treaty–based organization, but is a framework process which is three–track. Track-1 (A) are activities discussed and addressed by member countries. Track-1 (B) or 1 (A)/2 are activities approved by ARF, and involving scholars and officials from member-states active in their personal capacity. Track-2 provides a non-governmental forum for academics, scholars and researchers to interact in their private capacity with a view to developing structured regional processes.

The ARF is the only forum for security co-operation in the Asia–Pacific region. ARF Ministerial meetings are characterised by an informal setting. The discussions are free–flowing and there is no formal statement or formal agenda.

Global and regional security issues, as well as disarmament and non-proliferation issues constitute the agenda. The ARF sprit of CONSENSUS and DIALOGUE (MUFAKAT and MUSHAWARA), guides these discussions.

At the conclusion of the ARF meetings a Chairman's statement is issued this is not a "negotiated text", but tends to sum up the "broad consensus" emerging out of the discussions report on activities of the past years are considered and a "Programme of Work" for the next year approved.

In recent years the increased focus within ARF is on promoting cooperation against international terrorism. There is an ARF Inter-Sessional Meeting (ISM) on Counter-Terrorism and Transnational Crime (ISM on CT-TC). Other Inter-Sessional activities are:—

1. CBMs/Confidence Building Measures)
2. Disaster Relief
3. Transnational Organised Crime
4. Maritime Cooperation
5. Training for Peace – Keeping Operations

The Bangkok ASEAN Summit in December 1995 made India a full-dialogue partner of ASEAN. It was a conscious acknowledgement of India's "Look East Policy". India was invited to the ARF – Post Ministerial Conference Meetings (PMCs) from 1996, at the third ARF at Jakarta, Indonesia. Admission to the ARF underlines the acceptance of India's role and position in the Asia–Pacific region.

India sees the ARF as an experiment for fashioning of a new pluralistic, cooperative security order in tune will the diversity of the Asia-Pacific region, both in politico-security and economic spheres, and underlines the commitment of India to the objective of sustaining regional peace and stability.

India participates regularly in meetings of the Inter-Sessional Support Group (ISG) on CBMs (Confidence Building Measures).

The MEA (Ministry of External Affairs) and MOD (ministry of Defence) and interested academicians are involved in ARF discussions.

Although ASEAN has under taken the obligation to be the primary driving force of the ARF, a successful ARF requires the active participation and cooperation of all participants. ARF must be always sensitive to, and take into account the interests and concerns of all ARF participants.

It would be unwise for a young and fragile process like the ARF, to tackle all challenges simultaneously. An evolutionary approach is required. This evolution can take place in three stages –

Stage 1 – Promotion of CBMs.

Stage 2 – Development of Preventive Diplomacy Measures (PD).

Stage 3 – Development of Conflict – Resolution Mechanisms.

The ARF must be accepted as a "sui generis" organisation. It has no established precedents to follow. A great deal of innovation and ingenuity will be required to keep ARF moving forward, while at the same time ensuring that it enjoys the support of its diverse participants. This is a major challenge both for ASEAN countries and other ARF participants. The UN Secretary General's "Agenda for Peace" has recognised that just as no two regions or situations are the same, so the design of cooperative work and its division of labour must adjust to the realities of each case with flexibility and creativity".

A list of ARF Meetings and Venues, since inception is given below—

1. 1st ARF—Bangkok, Thailand, July 1994.

2. 2nd ARF—Bander Seri Begawan, Brunei Darussalam, August 1995.
3. 3rd ARF—Jakarta, Indonesia, July 1996 (*Myanmar and India become Members*).
4. 4th ARF - Subang Jaya, Malaysia, 27th July 1997.
5. 5th ARF - Manila, the Philippines, 27th July 1998.
6. 6th ARF - Singapore, 26th July 1999.
7. 7th ARF - Bangkok, Thailand, 27th July 2000.
8. 8th ARF - Hanoi, Vietnam, 25th July 2001.
9. 9th ARF - Bandar Seri Begawan, Brunei Darussalam, 31st 2002.
10. 10th ARF - Cambodia, 18th June 2003.
11. 11th ARF - Jakarta, Indonesia 2nd July 2004, *(Pakistan becomes a member)*
12. 12th ARF - Vientiane, Laos, 29th July 2005
13. 13th ARF - Kuala Lumpur, Malaysia, 28th July 2006, *(Bangladesh)*
14. 14th ARF - (To be held) at the Philippines on 27th August 2007.

The Twenty-six member – States of ARF (ie ARF participants) as of Jan 2007 are:—

1. Australia
2. Bangladesh
3. Brunei
4. Cambodia
5. Canada
6. China
7. European Union
8. India
9. Indonesia

10. Japan
11. North Korea
12. South Korea
13. Laos
14. Malaysia
15. Mongolia
16. Myanmar
17. New Zealand
18. Pakistan
19. Papua New Guinea
20. The Philippines
21. Russia
22. Singapore
23. Thailand
24. Timor
25. Vietnam
26. United States

Role of Important Member – Countries of ARF in the Forum

To put issues in proper perspective, the role of important member-countries of ASEAN needs to be assessed. The ASEAN countries may have differences on the questions of regional security and bilateral tensions may surface periodically, but the ASEAN states are in agreement that ARF has by and large met their expectations. ASEAN states prefer to keep the Chairmanship of ARF within ASEAN. The idea of sharing the Chairmanship of ARF with non–ASEAN states, with a view to pro -actively engage major powers like the US has been more or less dismissed by ASEAN.Considering their preoccupation with domestic, political security and economic challenges, ASEAN members favour maintaining the status-quo.

ASEAN states are generally satisfied with the current CBMs that are in progress, and would like then to be continued. Many ASEAN states are not in agreement to move to the phase of " preventive diplomacy" with Vietnam and Malaysia voicing their apprehensions. More ASEAN states also see no merit in the idea of establishing an ARF secretariat as creating formal structures goes against the grain of the ASEAN way.

Japan

Japan recognises that the ARF has established habits of dialogue among member countries, However, Japan has expressed reservations as the ARF's evolutionary approach and decision-making by consensus. Tokyo has argued that this could work against the Forum's ability to respond effectively to regional contingencies. Concerning future directions, among the three North East Asian countries, Japan has been most local in supporting the idea of pushing the "preventive diplomacy " agenda forward in the ARF.

China

The Chinese attitude towards ARF has evolved significantly. Its initial suspicions of the ARF as a possible tool of American "containment", and for its smaller neighbours to "gang up" against Chinese interests, and its territorial claims have substantially lessened. Beijing has found the ARF useful in articulating its own security perspectives, and reassuring its neighbours about its strategic intentions.

Australia

Australia views the ARF as having made an important contribution to regional security. It has been especially active in the ARFs work on transnational crime, such as money laundering and the trafficking of drugs, people and small arms.

United States (US)

The US views the ARF as not having made much progress. Yet, Washington never expected the Forum to move fast on concrete issues. The "development of a habit of discussion and some consensus on process" was deemed as the only realistic expectation over the medium term. In regard to future directions, the US maintains realistic expectations of the ARF, being fully aware of the Forum's limitations.

In the light of the events of 9-11-2001 and their enormous impact on American security thinking, the US would likely want the ARF to strengthen cooperation in the fight against, terrorism through the ARF – ISG work on transnational crime. The US also supports the continued ASEAN chairmanship of ARF.

Russia

Russia has been perceived as not really an active player in the ARF, and its expectations of ARF should therefore most likely be modest. Nevertheless, Russia has of late played an active role (together with ASEAN) in drafting the "Declaration on Principles Guiding Mutual Relations in the Asia – Pacific" (the Pacific Concord). Russia sees the Forum as a multilateral mechanism that reinforces the peace efforts of other multilateral ventures, for example, the six party talks on the Korean Peninsula.

European Union (EU)

In the post – 9/11 strategic milieu, the EU recognises the potential role that ARF can play in addressing some of the more urgent issues, such as terrorism and transnational crime. In the past, the EU's participation in the ARF has been linked or confined to the country holding, the EU's presidency. With is new "Common Foreign and Security Policy" (CFSP); EU participation in the ARF could be increased to three members. With the EU's experience in building multilateral security institutions, joint sharing of experience and expertise between EU and the ARF–particularly with regard to developing and consolidating CBMs and preventive diplomacy mechanisms would be most useful.

INDIA and the ARF

India values its membership of the ARF. It sees in ARF an experiment for the fashioning of a new pluralistic, cooperative security order in tune with the diversity of the Asia –Pacific region and in consonance with the transition away from a world characterised by poles built around military alliances. Though ARF covers a broad geographic spectrum, India believes it is built around the nucleus of ASEAN and is ASEAN-driven. Our participation in ARF demonstrates India's increasing pro-active engagement in the Asia-Pacific region, both in the politico-security and economic spheres. It also underlines India's commitment to the objective of sustaining regional peace and stability.

When India became a member of the ARF in July 1996, it hoped that it will be an adequate forum to protect and project India's security and strategic interests in the ASEAN and larger Asia -Pacific region. It was hoped that as Pakistan was not a member of ARF consultations, contentious Indo-Pak and Intra- SAARC issues would not be raised, and stymie the functioning of ARF. However, Pakistan became a member of the ARF in July 2004. India hoped that Islamabad would adhere to its commitment of not raising Kashmir or any other disputable Indo-Pak issues at the Asia-Pacific's only security grouping. It is to Pakistan's credit that it has not brought contentious Indo-Pak issues in ARF proceedings. With Bangladesh also becoming a member of ARF, India's hope is that ARF will keep out contentious sub-continental issues from ARF proceedings.

India has been an active participant in various ARF processes, and has hosted several ARF—related activities.

Some of the important ARF—related events hosted by India are:—

1. Anti – piracy workshop in Mumbai, organised by the Indian Coast Guard in conjunction with MEA and MOD in 2000.
2. ARF – Inter-Sessional Grouping (ISG) on CBMs co- chaired with Vietnam, 2001.
3. ARF workshop on Maritime Security Challenges, co-chaired with US, Mumbai 2003.
4. ARF Heads of Defence Colleges and Institutions, New Delhi, 2003.
5. Workshop on Training for Co-operative Maritime Security and Cyber Security, 2005.

6. Workshop on Cyber Security, 2006.

Forthcoming Seminar in on "ARF and UN – Challenges and Prospects" later this year at a venue in India.

Achievements of ARF

Despite the great diversity of the membership of ARF, the forum has attained a record of achievements that have contributed to the maintenance of peace, security and cooperation in the region. Some of the important achievements of ARF are:

1. The usefulness of ARF as a venue for multilateral and bilateral dialogue, and consultations and the establishment of effective principles for dialogue and co-operation in decision-making by consensus, non- interference, incremental progress and moving at a pace comfortable to all.
2. The willingness among ARF participants to discuss a wide range of security issues in a multilateral setting.
3. The mutual confidence gradually built by cooperative activities.
4. The cultivation of habits of dialogue and consultation on political and security issues.
5. The transparency promoted by such ARF measures as the exchange of information relating to defence policy, and the publication of defence white papers and lastly,
6. The networking developed among national security, defence and military officials of ARF participants.

In conclusion, ARF has provided a good platform for INDIA to participate in multi-lateral security and strategic issues in the ASEAN and wider Asia-Pacific region.

INDEX